FROM
PRINCIPLES
TO
PROFIT

FROM
PRINCIPLES
TO
PROFIT

THE ART OF MORAL MANAGEMENT

PAUL PALMAROZZA
CHRIS REES

ARCTURUS

Dedication
To our wives Judica and Valery, for their loving support.

Arcturus Publishing Limited
26/27 Bickels Yard
151–153 Bermondsey Street
London SE1 3HA

Published in association with
foulsham
W. Foulsham & Co. Ltd,
The Publishing House, Bennetts Close, Cippenham,
Slough, Berkshire SL1 5AP, England

ISBN-13: 978-0-572-03192-3
ISBN-10: 0-572-03192-0

This edition printed in 2006
Copyright © 2006 Paul Palmarozza & Chris Rees/
Arcturus Publishing Limited

British Library Cataloguing-in-Publication Data: a catalogue record for this
book is available from the British Library

Printed in Finland

CONTENTS

Introduction

Chapter One: *The Role of Business in Society*   12

Chapter Two: *Values*   42

Chapter Three: *Morality and Virtue*   54

Chapter Four: *Advocates of the Moral Way*   74

Chapter Five: *Principles – the Foundation of a Business*   90

Chapter Six: *Universal Principles at Work – Truth*   106

Chapter Seven: *Universal Principles at Work – Love*   126

Chapter Eight: *Other Universal Principles at Work*   146

Chapter Nine: *Service, the Heart of Business*   172

Chapter Ten: *Creativity and Loving your Work*   200

Chapter Eleven: *The Moral Manager:*
Leader, Organizer, Teacher   216

Chapter Twelve: *Moral Management in Practice*   234

Chapter Thirteen: *The Way Forward*   252

References   266

Bibliography   274

Index   284

INTRODUCTION

W hy would two busy people decide to write yet another book about business when the shelves of bookshops are already filled with business publications telling us how to succeed in three, seven or ten easy steps?

Having both worked in business for forty years, we have learned at least one important lesson: the time to act is when you see a clear, explicit need in the market *and* when you believe that what you have to offer helps meet that need.

We perceive such a need – to remind those of you in business of the benefits of principled and ethical actions for yourself, for those whom you manage, for your company, customers, shareholders and the community and to suggest ways in which these benefits may be realized.

You do not have to be especially astute to notice that 'something is rotten' in the state of our business community. Although most businessmen are honest and upright, the numerous examples of dishonesty, greed and corruption that leap out of the pages of the newspapers make it clear that trust in business and business people is at a dangerously low ebb. This has affected not only the more affluent countries like the USA, UK, France and Germany but also the rapidly developing countries such as China, Russia and India.

As trust in business leaders erodes, the willingness of people to continue investing their savings in the stock market also comes under question. The implications of such a withholding of funds have already caused a dramatic response from many governments, in the form of yet more regulation, as any reduction in available capital could destabilize their entire economic infrastructure.

What the two of us have experienced in business, in addition to the greed of an active minority, is the good that comes from working together with colleagues in a shared partnership to build a successful business. We have seen how a business can begin by serving a real need in society. Through the application of intelligence, care and plain hard work by a cohesive and dedicated team, you can gradually attract a loyal customer base and well-motivated staff. Then profit flows in naturally. As your reputation grows, self-confidence is developed so that other people decide they would like to invest in or work for the company.

The great opportunity to engage in a worthwhile enterprise is being undermined by an increasingly sceptical, even cynical, view of business. Consequently, young people may well seek other ways to express their natural talents.

Business at its best is an instrument for the creation of wealth for the benefit of all, wealth that can be used for the common good. When business flourishes the fruits can be used to improve the working of society, including developments in culture and education as well as general prosperity and well-being. These lofty aims are well worth the effort of pursuing them.

Both the potential and the problems are widely recognized and increasingly well documented. In attempting to address the need for a new direction, we shall present a perspective that considers the lessons learned from history as well as an analysis of current conditions. We shall look at the moral issues as well as the economic results and examine the impact of our actions on ourselves, our families, the community and society overall.

It seems important, as concerned members of the business community, that we demonstrate not only that the selfish actions of a few are damaging all those engaged in enterprise, but also that there is a better way to do business; one that is based on the fine principles of life, and which, when put into practice, will be profitable for all concerned. The events of recent years have provoked considerable discussion on subjects such as moral values, business ethics and corporate social responsibility (CSR). According to critics, some views have come across as too 'righteous' without reference to the practicalities of business life, while others have justified the pragmatic approach at the expense of moral values. We hope to strike a better balance and to offer some practical suggestions on how to tread a path that embraces both principles and profits.

What experience do we have to call on? Paul holds a BSEE (Elec Eng) from the New Jersey Institute of Technology (USA), and an MBA from Drexel University (USA). He has worked in business for more than forty years, first for Control Data Corporation in the USA and Europe in sales and marketing management roles and then as General Manager of a European businesses unit. After a sabbatical year at Oxford University, where he gained a Diploma in Education Studies, he began a new phase of his career in the UK as a self-employed consultant in his chosen field of technology-based training, now called e-learning. Eighteen years ago he founded a company focusing on financial awareness training for managers in industry. In 2001 the company was listed on the AIM market as Intellexis PLC with Paul as Chief Executive. Since that time the company has made several acquisitions and is now called the ILX Group. Paul is now President of the Intellexis business unit, helping to establish global partnerships in China, India and Brazil.

Chris graduated from the University of St Andrews with an MA in Logic and Metaphysics and Political Economy. He has been in business for forty years, beginning with IBM in technical and training roles. He worked for a computer time-sharing company in the USA in the early 1970s in systems and product management. Returning to the UK, he joined Logica, the IT systems company and rose through systems, consulting and product management roles to be Managing Director of Logica Software Products Ltd. He then spent eleven years as a Partner with Deloitte Consulting, advising finance industry clients in the UK, Russia and Eastern Europe. He left Deloitte in 1996 to co-found Charteris, a business consulting company specializing in providing a bridge between business and technology. Charteris was listed on AIM in 2000. Chris is an Executive Director of Charteris plc, a practising management consultant and an expert in IT disputes.

In addition to our family and business activities, we have also both been studying practical philosophy for a similar period as members of the School of Economic Science, a London-based educational charity which has been running courses in economics and philosophy since 1937. Philosophy, the love of wisdom, is that ancient and modern study which attempts to discover the first principles, the fundamental laws governing a subject and then to apply them. For example, the understanding and application of the first principles of law could result in one becoming a wise lawyer. We believe that the same applies in business. One can become a wise businessman or businesswoman.

As part of our philosophical studies we have attempted to understand and put into practice the key principles of life as they apply to business activities. For the last three years we have run evening courses in Philosophy in Business, where these issues have been explored with business people of all ages, experience and seniority. The pressing questions expressed by these groups have been:

Can I work in business according to true principles *and* still be successful?
and
If yes, then *how*?'

These are real questions and the need is for each of us to answer them for ourselves. Our aim therefore is to help others to formulate a personal and appropriate response. It is our firm conviction that the answer to the first question is 'yes', and therefore a good part of our offering explores practical ways in which this may be brought about. While making no claim to wisdom, we have had some useful personal insights and experiences, which we offer together with words of wisdom from teachers representing various cultures along with commentary and observations by numerous business people, in the hope that they may be of some benefit to you.

We shall explore the conditions conducive to personal development and to good business that are created when principles and profits are in harmony. We shall examine how the quality of service offered is enhanced; how creativity can arise naturally in response to the need and how working for the common good expands one's own happiness as well as that of others. We shall also look at how, when shared common values become a living reality in an organization, trust, loyalty and productivity thrive and how this environment allows for the fuller expression of individual talents and the flourishing of effective leadership.

There is obviously no neat single answer. While the principles are unchanging, the unique solution for now, for this time and place, must be discovered. This will be easier if the principles are known and then tested in practice. Another necessary ingredient, if the effort is to be sustained, is good company in the form of other kindred souls who are interested in the same quest and willing to work. We have already discovered a large number of like-minded people in all parts of the world, walking in the same direction. Some of their experiences are included in the book. We are confident that if you embark on this road, you too will find like-minded people with whom to share your journey.

We have drawn upon our own experiences to illustrate many of the points we make. The work is a joint product, and therefore we have written it in the first person plural, but we have used the first person singular when it is an individual experience.

From Principles to Profit points the direction. We hope that you will find the venture profitable at all levels.

CHAPTER 1 - THE ROLE OF BUSINESS

B usiness, commerce or trade is an integral part of any society. Some individuals or groups of people have, due to their nature or to geographical necessity, given greater emphasis to this activity. Business exists in society because individuals have a wide range of talents and needs and it is not practical for everyone to provide for all their own needs and desires, including such necessities as food, housing and clothing.

Therefore from the earliest days of organized society various specialities emerged. Some people were more suited to work the land to produce food; those with talent for building made shelters or produced tools while others made clothing. The need thus arose for a means to trade the fruits of each other's production. This exchange of the fruits of individual talents is the basis for business.

As societies became larger and more spread out, and as the variety of products and services required by the populace expanded, some people naturally began to specialize in facilitating this exchange of goods. As this activity became the basis of their individual livelihood, it was necessary that enough benefit accrued to the trader in terms of the goods traded, or later when money was introduced, sufficient profit to purchase the goods necessary for the trader and his family. Thus profit is a natural consequence of business in society and essential to its operation.

As with any such activity, business must be sanctioned by society and given licence to operate. Being given this right brings with it corresponding duties and responsibilities to society. As societies

IN SOCIETY

have become more complex and dispersed it has been necessary to formalize the rules of engagement for business. For these activities to flourish a supportive atmosphere is required that in turn depends on the public's attitude to business. We shall consider the question of the role of business in society initially from an historical perspective, because the attitudes and values that we have inherited play an important part in forming current ideas and attitudes to business.

But before embarking on this, it is also necessary to consider the key factors that are most conducive to trade at any particular time. There are five main considerations:

- STABILITY: peace between trading partners that permits the free flow of goods.
- TRANSPORT: the means to transport goods and services in a timely and cost-effective manner.
- DESIRE: the demand for the goods of another. This requires some knowledge of the existence of the goods, some experience of their value, possibly an acquired taste to have them again and again and a lack of an equivalent product at a competitive price available within one's own domain.
- MEANS OF EXCHANGE: either through the medium of money or through the bartering of goods and services.
- FREEDOM: the ability to trade freely without excessive intervention by government agencies for financial, legal or security reasons.

As we shall see in our historical review, the degree to which these conditions are met in a society determines the extent of trade. These factors also influence ideas about business. For example, when there is strong desire in one country for the goods of another country and the merchants are successful in making the desired products available at a reasonable price, then these merchants will most likely be both well considered and well rewarded. The reputation of business rises.

If demand becomes excessive and supply is inadequate, then that situation may encourage greed on the part of the merchants so that they go beyond the bounds of morality either in obtaining the goods or, when obtained, in offering them at exorbitant prices. The reputation of business in general then suffers and corrective factors are applied in the form of more stringent laws and severe punishments.

So the two extremes of society's view of business are that business is either an appropriate and necessary activity of society or that it is inherently wrong or sinful, inevitably linked to greed and corruption.

One can find an early reference to this debate in Aristotle (384–322 BC), who declared that:

> . . . the life of money-making is undertaken under compulsion and wealth is evidently not the good we are seeking; for it is merely useful for the sake of something else.
>
> Aristotle, *Nicomachean Ethics*, 1995 edn.

Ancient Jewish law made clear references to business, which in Judaism is neither sinful nor disreputable, provided that it is conducted morally. Of the 613 commandments in the Pentateuch, the observance of which is incumbent on male Jews, 100 are concerned with money and business and by comparison only twenty-eight deal with dietary laws and seven with Sabbath observance.

Christian thinkers in the third and fourth centuries were among the most powerful critics of business. They identified the wealth accumulation and greed associated with business as the prime source of the corruption that had contributed to the fall of Rome.

Certain trades also were condemned as being 'unclean' or 'impure', unfit for Christians. At the root of this approach was the belief that a Christian should concentrate on preparing his soul for the life to come. To focus on the things of the world was to be distracted from the real purpose of existence.

In reviewing the past, one does find useful parallels that if properly assessed can shine light on the present. In this way one can learn from history rather than just repeating it. For example, for those of us living in the twenty-first century there does seem to be much to be learned from the conditions that existed in society during the latter stages of the Roman Empire in the fourth and fifth centuries. The historian Edward Gibbon, in the *Decline and Fall of the Roman Empire* (1977 edn.), summed up the state of the empire at that time in five characteristics that he claimed were common to all dying cultures:

- Extravagant display of wealth and outward show;
- Growing disparity between rich and poor;
- Unhealthy obsession with sex;
- Decline in military discipline;
- Universal desire to live off the bounty of the state.

Do they sound familiar?

The Middle Ages

In the 6th century a book was written which was to become one of the most widely read in Europe for the next thousand years: *The Consolation of Philosophy*, by Boethius (1998 edn.), a very wealthy and influential Roman. He was appointed *Magister Officium* (Head of Government) by King Theodoric the Great. But he fell from favour with the King, all his wealth was seized, he was arrested on charges of treason, imprisoned and later executed. While in prison he was visited by a personification of Philosophy who guided him through a reflection on his current state.

She, for Philosophy was a woman, told him, 'the real source of your current unhappiness is that you have forgotten your true nature'. She then led him through a reasoned exploration of the question, 'Are wealth, power, fame and pleasure the source of your **real happiness**?' His conclusion, after careful self-examination, was that while they were highly valued in the society in which he lived, the acquisition and attempted maintenance of these transient goals would not lead to the unchanging happiness that is the heritage of all human beings. Once Boethius grasped this, he was ready to rediscover his true nature, one full of love, knowledge and bliss. The book concludes with this advice from Philosophy: 'Avoid vice, therefore cultivate virtue.' This advice is an excellent reminder of the importance of virtues and values that had been forgotten in Roman times.

In the early Middle Ages disdain for worldy things was prevalent. This attitude was known as *contemptus mundi* (contempt for the world). It was formulated as a doctrine by Pope Innocent III in *De Contemptu Mundi* in 1216 (cit. in Geary, 1977). It begins, 'Man was formed of dust, slime and ashes,' and it goes on to inveigh in colourful language against the sins of the flesh and the misery of the human condition. Innocent asks, 'Of what advantage, then, are riches, food, and honours? For riches will not free us from death, neither food protect us from the worm nor honours from the stench.' This doctrine was prevalent for much of the Middle Ages and very much affected attitudes towards business life and business people.

Among the most significant forces in the conduct of business in the Middle Ages was the Guild. Guilds were formed as early as the ninth and tenth centuries in England, France and the Low Countries, and in the twelfth century in Germany. They started as lay confraternities primarily for the protection and common support of members of a particular trade. Guilds always had a strong religious element, often with their own patron saint and church. They developed into a combination of a trade union and a cartel, setting and protecting standards of conduct, and organizing the training of apprentices. They regulated weights and measures and the quality of goods, and controlled entry into the trade as well as the level of imports. They also set wages and working conditions.

In London where the guilds were most highly developed, the liverymen who controlled them also played a major role in the government of the City, as they elected the Lord Mayor and the Court of Common Council. At their best they were a strong moral force for good, though inevitably there were abuses in a system which lasted many hundreds of years. Their commitment to education, the development of skills in their trades and to charitable works lives on in the Livery Companies of the City of London.

One example of the moral force of the guilds is found in *Some Rules for the Conduct of Life*, (Livery Companies of the City of London, undated) a book that was given to each of us when we became Freemen of the City of London. The first three rules set out for the Freemen are summed up thus:

> Let the end you aim at be always good, be vigorous in making use of the proper means for the compassing of such an end; and in doing this be always very circumspect. If you proceed after this manner, you will certainly obtain the great end you propose to yourself in the life to come; and, if you fall short of some things which you desire in this world, you will have this comfort, that God thinks fit to deny them to you, not for any fault of yours, but for other good reasons, which he knows though you do not.

In the later Middle Ages and into the fourteenth and fifteenth centuries the general attitude towards business in the West was that reasonable profits were justifiable provided the business contributed to the greater good. A picture was formed of the good merchant – fair, honest, transparent in business dealings and devoted to God rather than commerce.

A notable example from this period is the teaching of San Bernardino of Siena (1380–1444). Unusually for a mendicant friar, San Bernardino spoke practically on subjects such as business ethics and usury. He saw business as a perfectly legitimate activity, where it performed a useful social function. Making a profit was legitimate but only insofar as it was incidental and not the prime purpose of business activity. He preached particularly against those who conspired to withhold supplies from the market place in order to drive prices up, especially in times of dearth. (He lived at a time when memory of the Black Death was still fresh and when regular out-breaks of one plague or another contributed to great poverty and disruption.) For San Bernardino there were four key aspects to business leadership: diligence or efficiency, responsibility, labour, and, remarkably, a willingness to assume risks. Through his preaching and travelling San Bernardino ensured the spread of these important ideas (*see* de Roover, 1967).

The Renaissance

The Renaissance philosopher Marsilio Ficino (1433–1499), whose patrons were the bankers Cosimo de' Medici and later his grandson Lorenzo de' Medici (Lorenzo the Magnificent), described the essential duties of a merchant as 'with true faith and diligence to nourish both the state and himself with good things from abroad'. (Ficino, 1984 edn.) A tradition of patronage also grew up in this period that saw business supporting different aspects of society, including church and state, in a substantial way: art, education and the relief of poverty.

Between the sixteenth and twentieth centuries the debate continued. Shakespeare's *Merchant of Venice*, written at the end of the sixteenth century, was much concerned with the business of the time. The plot is founded on the risks that the Christian merchant Antonio takes with his trading vessels, his desire to borrow from the Jewish moneylender Shylock and Bassanio's need of money in his suit of the wealthy Portia. Everything revolves around money. Of course there are many subtleties in the play and many possible interpretations, but this was one of the first plays that dwelt on how business operates. While most commentators focus on the explicit anti-Semitism in the play, the oppression of the Jews and other moral issues, a central tenet of the pound of flesh bargain is the sanctity of a contract in mercantile Venice.

The Industrial Revolution

During the eighteenth century, with the rush of democratic ideas in Europe, new possibilities for wealth creation were appearing and new problems were being encountered. In a contemporary commentary on business, the French philosopher, Baron de Montesquieu (1689–1755) wrote:

> True it is that when a democracy is founded on commerce, private people may acquire vast riches without the corruption of morals. This is because the spirit of commerce is naturally attended with that of frugality, economy, moderation, labour, prudence, tranquillity, order and rule. So long as that spirit subsists, the riches it produces have no bad effect. The mischief is when excessive wealth destroys the spirit of commerce, then it is that the inconveniences of inequality begin to be felt.
>
> Cit. in *Porcupines-A Philosophical Anthology*, Higgin, ed., 1999

However Montesquieu's optimism was not fully justified. The industrial revolution in Britain, the period from about 1780 to 1830, saw the rapid industrialization of Britain. It was followed a little later in other countries. This period saw a series of radical technological developments in spinning, weaving, steam power generation, railways, shipping and other fields. This in turn led to Britain becoming a leading world power, able to finance a powerful navy which could ensure the safety of its growing merchant shipping fleet, defend the Empire and further fuel Britain's growth as an economic power. It also led to a massive increase in the population and to a significant rise in the overall standard of living as well as the creation of a class of wealthy entrepreneurs.

The best of these, such as the Cadburys of Bournville and the Frys of York took their responsibilities to their workers very seriously, providing good quality accommodation and other amenities. However for many employers workers were seen as expendable tools of production, to be paid minimum wages and afforded no security of employment. This frequently led to poverty and destitution. Many were also cavalier about the effect their industries had on the environment and on the social fabric. Urban squalor, despoiled landscapes and dislocated communities were part of the price paid. Furnaces and forges blackened buildings, industrial chemicals and sewage killed off rivers, and roads and railways cut through fields and ancient monuments. Workers either migrated far from friends and family or suffered the de-skilling of their trade. Not even the skilled elite of the working class was immune from the insecurity of unemployment, illness and old age.

The twentieth century

The status of dominant economic power gradually passed from the Britain to the USA at the end of the nineteenth and early twentieth centuries. This power was based on the effective harnessing of technology and its application in the development of the most efficient manufacturing-based economy in the world. With much of Europe decimated by the destructive Great War of 1914-1918 and America's burst of prosperity in the 1920s, America began to distance itself from its European competitors. The depression of the

1930s brought in sober reminders about the cycles of boom and bust which are ignored at one's peril; however, this downturn was only temporary for the thriving American economy. With the end of global military conflicts in the 1940s the flourishing US manufacturing industry shifted from heavy emphasis on armaments, planes and ships to automobiles, industrial machinery and consumer goods, while still retaining a substantial defence production.

In the last quarter of the century another powerhouse came on the scene: Japan. The Japanese carefully observed the manufacturing techniques of the Americans and then went one better, especially in their attention to quality. By the late 1980s they had become the world's second largest economic power, a position they still hold despite a decade of stagnation.

The growing complexity of business stimulated the emergence of another trend, the rise of professionally trained managers and a body of knowledge on management theory and techniques. These developments gave greater credibility to business as a professional career and a growth in respect for individuals in the field. The Masters in Business Administration (MBA) degree became a base credential for aspiring business leaders. Here again the USA led the way with hundreds of colleges and business schools offering these degrees as early as the 1960s.

In the UK there were only a few educational institutions offering such a degree in the 1970s though this number grew rapidly until there were more than a hundred in the 1990s. Business school graduates began to receive equal recognition with other graduates with advanced degrees. Given the growing complexities of business, the in-depth knowledge possessed by MBAs became highly valued, and with this increased status came significant earnings.

Competition was keen and success came to be very highly valued. Business people continued to be generally well respected until the very end of the twentieth century when the speculative bubble of the dot.coms, and the huge expansion of telecommunications investment to support them, caught the fancy of the world. For a period of three to four years everyone seemed to be consumed in finding ways to hop on to the dot-com bandwagon. Reason was in short supply, replaced by clever get-rich-quick schemes and speculative gambles. Greed became the rule rather than the exception. The inevitable bursting of the bubble led to the revelation of massive frauds founded on the expectation of unlimited growth and the concomitant need to ensure that share prices continued to rise. When the growth stopped the schemes collapsed, and trust and confidence in business became seriously eroded.

Nobody should have been surprised as the whole episode was a repeat of the South Sea Bubble fraud of the early 1700s. There is nothing new about greed or gullibility. Sir Isaac Newton, who lost over £20,000 in the Bubble, wrote:

> I can calculate the motions of heavenly bodies, but not the madness of people.
>
> Isaac Newton, cit. in Mackay, *Extraordinary Popular Delusions and the Madness of Crowds*, 1995

The twenty-first century

A major factor in assessing the role of business in society today is that business has become a multi-cultural global operation. With the advent of global communications facilities, Internet trading, access to manufacturing and service resources in places like China and India, and the rapid transportation of agricultural produce from distant lands, the world is truly the marketplace.

This global expansion has cultural and ethical consequences. For an increasing number of businesses, large and small, there is no longer a single set of moral values or ethical standards. In fact, in many societies the reduced influence of religious teaching as the source of values and the guide for behaviour has caused even greater confusion. As we shall discuss later, for many people the basis of ethical judgements is bound up in the myriad local, regional, national and international laws and regulations that have been developed. Even for the well-informed this massive bureaucracy creates an unsettling doubt as to what is the correct course of action, as well as imposing a complexity and cost burden that inevitably affects everyone in society.

When conducting business with members of radically different cultures such as between Western companies and those of the Far East, the gulf can be wide. For example, in some Eastern societies it is the practice to become friends first before establishing a formal business relationship. The initial 'courting phase' involves the giving of gifts; meetings in the form of dinners and visits are arranged to put the other party at ease, meetings that are designed to allow the two parties to get to know each other.

The aim is to decide whether one is able to trust the other before committing to a long-term relationship. Once the friendship is established and the business arrangement is secured then it is expected that when problems arise, they will be faced together, much as one would in a good marriage.

Paul writes:

Recently I was working with a Chinese company with the aim that they would become our exclusive representative in China. They would in fact use our company name as well, so we had to be sure that they were the right organization. Their chairman visited the UK on several occasions, and I made two visits to China to see their operation at first hand. I had met members of the chairman's family and all the key executives from their company. There were the ritual banquets during my visit and they were very careful not to make me feel uncomfortable because of my vegetarian food requirements, and even overlooked the fact that I did not drink alcohol.

All this was a precursor to the actual contract negotiation which for the most part was conducted by telephone and e-mail. They proved to be very tough negotiators but we seemed to be moving step by step to a mutually agreeable solution. What changed the tone of our conversations was a desire on the part of our board to have the deal completed by the end of the year. The negotiation reached one stage where they were not moving at all on two crucial points, repeating over and over the same position. Due to the internal deadline I was forced to increase the pressure for a settlement. During one crucial phone conversation I heard the sound of my voice getting very sharp and the tone threatening. The response was one of palpable coolness and withdrawal. When the conversation ended I reflected on what had happened and on what I had learned about the importance that the Chinese placed on friendship and good relations between partners.

I asked myself the question, 'Would you speak to a friend in the way you just spoke to them?' The answer was clearly, no. The next day I called back and said that we had reached a difficult impasse and asked (as one would a friend), 'How can we resolve this issue?' The atmosphere changed and we were soon discussing a path to a compromise that was reached within a few days. The agreement was signed shortly before the New Year and as a goodwill gesture, they made their first payment the day after the agreement was signed.

We are still partners and although there have been difficult times along the way, we are both growing in understanding and mutual respect.

Compare this Eastern approach with the current Western approach which centres around lengthy negotiations aimed at producing a written contract that sets out in great detail all the possible eventualities and the conditions to which each party must adhere, with the consequences of non-performance also specified in great detail. This then becomes the basis of the business relationship.

Abuses are possible in both cases. Cleverly worded contracts can put one party at a serious disadvantage, while on the other hand the giving of gifts can easily become a form of bribery. When friendship becomes the key criterion then a partner may feel obliged to do the bidding of his friend, even if the action is illegal or viewed as immoral in that society.

In today's business environment we can observe many differences, such as the Islamic view of usury, that to lend money for interest is wrong, being at odds with Western approaches to finance; the acceptance of bribery as a necessary part of business in some societies; the disregard of intellectual property rights in others.

Are the diverse cultural differences too extensive to hope that some common ground might be found upon which a more harmonious relationship can be developed? In examining the various societies and the cultural values applied to business, we have been encouraged to find that the fundamental values are not so different even if their cultural values are very different. As the cultures of East and West have been isolated from each other for many centuries, clear differences in perspective have inevitably arisen. Despite the destructive, violent clashes of cultures observed in many parts of the world, there are some indications that increased trade may be the basis of new links being forged between East and West, North and South.

With the increased availability of information about other cultures, with access to affordable global transport that enables people to get a first-hand impression of other cultures and with the greater use of English as a common business language, business people are beginning to understand and appreciate each other better. The cultural differences, especially relating to moral values, do however need to be understood and respected.

Another key issue in the current business scene is trust – or the lack of it. With the bursting of the dot.com bubble at the beginning of the new millennium, a more sober view of business became established. It led to the appearance of a strong anti-capitalist movement and widely diverging views. Some people believe that the only truly ethical business is one that does not make a profit. At the other extreme there are those who believe that the primary duty of a company is simply to maximize value for the shareholders (and directors), which means maximizing profits above all. Is there a balanced position? Here is one view:

> The purpose of a business firm is not simply to make a profit, but is to be found in its very existence as a community of persons who in various ways are endeavouring to satisfy their basic needs, and who form a particular group at the service of the whole of society.
>
> Pope John Paul II, *In My Own Words*, 2005

In the next twenty to thirty years we may well see a shift in the culture of business to one more influenced by the traditions of the east, led by China, India and Japan. It is interesting to note that in the 1850s almost fifty per cent of world trade came from China and India; by the 1950s that figure had dropped to four to five per cent. It is now almost thirty per cent, and increasing dramatically (Overell, 2003).

Many forecast that the BRICs (Brazil, Russia, India, China) plus Japan will become the dominant economic power block after the USA, displacing the traditional European powers which have played this role in the past century. Their cultures and value systems will mean that business people in the West are going to have to adapt or they will find themselves at a serious competitive disadvantage.

Reflections on the past

With the economic globalization that has taken place over the last thirty to forty years, the practical interdependence of all countries is evident. While it has been generally accepted that the economic condition of a superpower like the USA can have a ripple effect throughout the world, it is now recognized that major problems or imbalances in other areas can also have a global impact. A financial crisis in Mexico can trigger a panic in Singapore; a threat to the supply of Middle East oil can dramatically increase world transport prices; the large, inexpensive yet productive workforce of China can eliminate manufacturing industries in highly developed Western countries.

Of late, considerable negative publicity has been voiced towards business practices that seem to indicate a determination to make profits regardless of the means. Activities that are deplored are those that contribute significantly to environmental pollution, that exploit child labour in developing countries, that charge exorbitant prices for medicines, that take unhealthy measures to maximize the yield of animals or agricultural land – the list goes on.

On the individual level there have been numerous cases of boards of directors and executive committee members voting themselves excessively generous compensation packages including large share options, while at the same time firing staff and cutting other costs. Cutting costs can help boost the share price which benefits the executives with share options, but it adds to the work pressures on the rest of the staff. Lay-offs may be necessary for the survival of the company, but if the pain is not shared, at least in part, by the executives, then a strong reaction is likely and reasonable. Business must be reminded that its role is to create wealth for the benefit of the entire community.

This type of behaviour is not characteristic of the majority, but it is sufficiently common in one form or another that there is growing distrust of the business community and a belief that business people are not acting responsibly. MORI (Market & Opinion Research International) began polling public attitudes to business in 1970 with the question, 'Do you agree that the profits of large companies help make things better for everyone who buys their goods and services?' In 1970 fifty-three per cent agreed. That number had steadily declined to twenty-five per cent in 1999, and that was before the recent spate of scandals associated with the dot.com bubble (Melville-Ross, 1999).

Spiritual influences

In all nations, East and West, philosophical and spiritual traditions have played a vital role in influencing the laws, ethics and moral values of society. The guidance has not always been followed and during those times when spiritual values and principles are forgotten or ignored, the negative impact on society can be clearly observed. We seem to be dangerously close to such a period.

Spiritual traditions have long described reality in rather different terms from those used by economic theories. While the latter are concerned with one aspect of human behaviour, i.e. economic actions, usually quantified in monetary terms, the spiritual view of reality is holistic, incorporating all the thoughts, words and deeds that make up our being and life.

In most economic and business textbooks human beings are seen as isolated consumers and producers, interacting in the market. The spiritual view puts this economic activity in the context of our desire for fulfilment as human beings, our need for truth, happiness and love. For these needs to be satisfied within the realm of business, we need to see that there is one life, one set of standards or principles to live by, and not different ways of behaving at home and at work. As long as there is an appreciation of one life and one standard of conduct, there will in fact be no conflict between the economic and the spiritual.

In the West the teachings of Plato have had an important impact on many of the key ideas and principles that govern society; for example our ideas about justice, equality or beauty. The other fundamental influence has been the Judaeo-Christian tradition, with special emphasis on the teachings of Bible and of Christ. The Ten Commandments of the Old Testament have been a primary influence on the structure of our legal system, and the Christian teachings on peace, virtue and love are still the basis for the moral and ethical values of many Western European, North American and Commonwealth countries.

In China the three main spiritual traditions of Confucianism, Buddhism and Taoism have each, in their turn, been the basis for the regulation of Chinese society. Probably the one with the most visible effect has been the teaching of Confucius (551–479 BC) that has permeated society. In fact, until the beginning of the twentieth century anyone who taught in a Chinese school had to demonstrate their intimate understanding of the Confucian principles of education. The advanced examinations for the Chinese civil service were based on the Confucian principles of good government. All aspects of Chinese society were influenced by Confucius, including the merchant class:

> To put the world in order, we must first put the nation
>   in order;
> To put the nation in order, we must first put the family
>   in order;
> To put the family in order, we must first cultivate our per-
>   sonal life and
> To cultivate our personal life, we must put our hearts right.
>   Confucius, *Analects* 1971 edn.

It is now becoming much clearer to Western business people how the Qu'ran and the teaching of Muhammad influence the conduct of those who follow the Islamic tradition. There are not only guidelines on that which is acceptable but also clear statements as to the duties and responsibilities of people engaged in commerce.

> He who is satisfying the desire of the heart will be rewarded
> by God provided the methods adopted are permissible.
>   *The Qur'an*, 1998 trans.

It is now being predicted that within the next twenty years India will follow China in a process of transformation from the status of a developing country to one of an economic powerhouse, within the top five in the world. It will become increasingly important if one wants to do business in India to appreciate how the great spiritual heritage of this nation continues to influence the values and mores of the people.

> When work is for the satisfaction of the individual and also
> the society – if both gain from its production and use – then
> it is righteous; and, if only the producer makes a gain at the

loss of society or nation, then it must be unrighteous. This principle applies to all times and all nations.

Sri Shantananda Saraswati, unpublished conversations

One common observation that is made about business throughout the ages is that it flourishes only where and when there is relative peace and stability. Indeed business invests only when there is the stability that peace brings. This can be seen from the early days of East–West trade along the Silk Road through the Middle East to and from India. When land routes were disrupted by a hostile phase of Turkish expansion, sea routes were opened up. And when spices from the Far East could not be brought from Byzantium to Venice by sea, they came overland through Romania and Germany. In recent times the massive growth in world trade can be easily traced to the relative peace that has obtained in the world since the end of the Second World War.

It is also observable that with the increase in wealth in a society, art and culture tend to flourish. This comes about mainly due to the patronage of the wealthy who spread their largesse through charitable activities. This 'giving back' to society some part of what one has earned is a natural response; however it is clearly not universal in its application.

Selfless activity is by no means the rule and in the normal cycle of life the selfless becomes the exception, giving way to selfish actions designed to maximize the benefit for 'me and mine'. It is during these periods of selfishness that the view of human nature takes a cynical turn. Looking after 'number one' becomes the norm and it can even reach the point where some people actually believe that 'greed is good', or if not exactly good, then at least normal.

Here in contrast is a view on how we can become rich 'naturally':

To produce without possessing,

To work without expecting,

To enlarge without usurping,

To know when you have enough is to be rich.

Lao Tse, *The Sayings of Lao Tse*, 1972 edn.

The waning influence of religion and growth in spirituality

It is clear from the dwindling attendance at religious services of all denominations that the positive influence exercised by organized religion in helping people make moral decisions has been on the wane for many years. The majority of the current generation under thirty years of age in developed Western countries have not had a solid grounding in the theory and practice of their family religion. As a result, the fine teachings regarding virtuous and moral action have not been adequately presented or discussed.

While the existing permissive atmosphere is not conducive to moral behaviour, there are definitely some positive influences: for instance, a growing interest in spirituality on the part of many young people. The void created by the lack of credible guidance from the established Western religions is in some cases being filled by the teachings and practices of Eastern philosophies, such as meditation, yoga and tai chi.

A notable characteristic of these philosophies, such as Buddhism or the Indian Vedic tradition, is the encouragement of exploration within, a search for true knowledge and happiness in one's being and not in the external, transient creation. These teachings do not require people to drop out of active participation in society. People are encouraged to concentrate on living a life based on true principles and not to be deceived by the 'fool's gold' of material success at any cost.

> Give up all cunning and deceit. Those who are engaged in business such as work in an office or trade, should stick to the truth.
>
> *The Gospel of Sri Ramakrishna*, 1980 edn.

Another problem area is the desire for immediate success. There will be a more detailed discussion of values in Chapter 2 but a story relating to this is appropriate here.

> Matajuro Yagyu was the son of a famous swordsman. His father, believing that his son's work was too mediocre to anticipate mastership, disowned him.
>
> So Matajuro went to Mount Futara and there found the famous swordsman Banzo. But Banzo confirmed the father's judgement. 'You wish to learn swordsmanship under my guidance?' asked Banzo. 'You cannot fulfil the requirements.'
>
> 'But if I work hard, how many years will it take me to become a master?' persisted the youth.
>
> 'The rest of your life,' replied Banzo.
>
> 'I cannot wait that long,' explained Matajuro. 'I am willing to pass through any hardship if only you will teach me. If only I become your devoted servant, how long might it be?'
>
> 'Oh, maybe ten years,' Banzo replied.
>
> 'My father is getting old, and soon I must take care of

him,' continued Matajuro. 'If I work far more intensively, how long would it take me?'

'Oh, maybe thirty years,' said Banzo.

'Why is that?' asked Matajuro. 'First you say ten and now thirty years. I will undergo any hardship to master this art in the shortest time!'

'Well,' said Banzo, 'In that case you will have to remain with me for seventy years. A man in such a hurry as you are to get results quickly seldom succeeds.'

'Very well,' declared the youth, understanding at last that he was being rebuked for impatience, 'I agree.'

Matajuro was told never to speak of fencing and never to touch a sword. He cooked for his master, washed the dishes, made the bed, cleaned the yard, cared for the garden, all without a word of swordsmanship.

Three years passed. Still Matajuro laboured on. Thinking of his future, he was sad. He had not even begun to learn the art to which he had devoted his life.

But one day Banzo crept behind him and gave him a terrific blow with a wooden sword. The following day, when Matajuro was cooking rice, Banzo again sprang upon him unexpectedly.

After that, day and night, Matajuro had to defend himself from the unexpected thrusts. Not a moment passed in any day that he did not have to think about the taste of Banzo's sword.

He learned so rapidly he brought smiles to the face of his master.

Matajuro became the greatest swordsman in the world.

'The Taste of Banzo's Sword' in *Zen Flesh, Zen Bones*, Reps (ed.) 1957

What are the main lessons from that story?

Success was obviously very important to Matajuro. That strong drive to succeed *in the shortest time* resonates strongly with life in the twenty-first century.

Banzo observed that someone with a desire for rapid success rarely attains it. Instead he counselled simple attention, obedience and readiness to meet the need of the moment.

One of the main causes of the growing lack of trust is the increasing tendency for business leaders to respond to the pressure for short-term gains, for meeting their performance targets, by resorting to actions that ignore moral or ethical values. Expediency becomes the driving factor. Getting the job done (at any cost) becomes the rule rather than the exception.

He that maketh haste to be rich shall not be innocent.

Proverbs, 28:20

Another topical example is in the world of sport that is fast becoming more of a business, with money and fame often the primary motivators for sportsmen. The numerous examples of athletes using performance-enhancing drugs and other deceptions are too pervasive to ignore.

A consequence of this desperate need for success is a willingness to say or do anything in order to improve one's chances of success. One individual who was accused of cheating in order to win a contract said that he knew what he was doing was wrong, but he did not think it was illegal. He was willing to go against his moral values in order to succeed, with the only 'possible' deterrent being a legal sanction. This is called secular moral relativism – 'If it's not illegal, it's okay'.

When success becomes the most important factor, then one also becomes subject to its corollary, failure. The fear of failure becomes equal in intensity to the desire for success. They are two sides of one coin. When there is fear of failure, one's thoughts, words and actions are all influenced. Firstly there will be a tendency to take on only those tasks where success is assured. This leads inevitably to limiting the scope of activity to familiar ground.

Attachment to success also results in a desire to be seen to be successful. Feeling this, a person needs to project an image of success and to display the trappings of success so as to gain the esteem of others as a result of the appearance of success. For a person with a strong desire for success, integrity and honesty are very likely to be compromised.

What are the typical measures of success in our society today?

Among the many surveys that have appeared recently in major European and US publications three stand out as reflecting those measures of success most generally esteemed. These surveys were:
- The 100 Richest People in the UK – i.e. material wealth;
- The 100 Sexiest Women – i.e. physical beauty of a certain type;
- The 100 Most Powerful People – i.e. power and status.

Liberally dispersed in these lists were stars of music and film, sportsmen and wealthy business executives. These have become the celebrities of our time. Their type of success seems to be very highly valued in Western society today. Notable in their absence from such lists are teachers, nurses and artists, people who make a vital contribution to the welfare of society.

The question that Philosophy asked Boethius arises once more: 'Are these material measures of success (fame, wealth, power) the source of lasting happiness?' As human beings we share the common desire for happiness. In fact, happiness is that which we all truly value and these other factors are simply a means to attain this happiness.

> All human beings seek the happy life, but many confuse the means, for example wealth and fame (status), with that life itself. This misguided focus on the means to a good life takes people further from the happy life. The really worthwhile things are the virtuous activities that make up the happy life, not the external means that may seem to produce it.
>
> Epictetus, *The Art of Living*, 1995 edn.

Instead of an increase in happiness resulting from more wealth, what is manifest in our society is a dramatic increase in the general level of stress and tension in both home and work-place. The *Independent* reported recently that more than twenty-five per cent of NHS prescriptions are for depression and other mental illnesses (*Independent*, 30 March 2004). This is neither surprising nor entirely new. Five hundred years ago Marsilio Ficino observed:

> Now, I have often noticed that a person who depends on external things always lives a disturbed and anxious life and suffers many a disappointment, while the only person to live in peace and certainty is the one who leads a life based, not upon the passing show without, but upon the eternal within himself.
>
> Marsilio Ficino, *Letters*, Vol. 2, 1984 edn.

The desperate striving for success without regard for the cost, the fast-paced environment, the grasping for transient values in a search for personal happiness are conditions that are not conducive to ethical or moral behaviour.

Indeed they lead directly to the vice often evident in business: greed. Greed is also not new. Here is an Egyptian's writing on the subject, which appeared over three thousand years ago:

> Do not be greedy lest your name stink.
>
> The wealth of the generous man is greater than the wealth
>   of the greedy.
>
> Greed puts strife and combat in the house.
>
> Greed removes shame, mercy and trust from the heart.
>
> Money is the snare the god has placed on the earth for the
>   impious man so that he should worry daily.
>
> He who gives food to the poor, the god takes him to himself
>   in boundless mercy.
>
> The goods of the greedy are ashes driven by the wind.
>
> *The Fifteenth Instruction* – ancient Egyptian text,
>   cit. in *Egyptian Wisdom*, Element Books, 1977

The spate of corporate horror stories based on greed is epitomized by Enron, the energy trading company that crashed in 2001. This led to the conviction on fraud charges and prison terms for a number of its executives, and the trial of others, ongoing as we write, and WorldCom, which survived its corruption scandal unlike its chief executive officer, Bernie Ebbers, who was given a long prison term for false accounting. These two scandals led to the collapse of the accounting firm Arthur Andersen. There were also corporate fraud scandals in Europe including that at Parmalat, the big dairy products company in Italy, BMW in Germany, and in the UK and the Netherlands Shell had to restate its oil reserves many times as the figures had been inflated. These examples may be taken by some as further indications that business cannot be trusted.

There are many other examples of senior executives who wanted to succeed at any cost and were willing to lie and cheat to achieve their ends. There are, too, examples of business activities just to make money that affront human dignity, such as the production of pornographic films.

One of the challenges in today's world, with its strong emphasis on measurable goals, is how to quantify non-material values such as happiness or well-being.

In the next three chapters, we shall look at the nature and types of values (Chapter Two); at morality, moral values and at the established practice of living a moral life which has come to be known as virtue (Chapter Three). We shall also briefly examine the moral guidance offered by the religions and philosophic traditions, as these are all advocates of the moral way (Chapter Four). In the succeeding chapters we shall then explore ways in which these values may be applied in the workplace and the resultant effects.

CHAPTER 2 - VALUES

I t is part of our nature as human beings that our actions are based upon values that guide the decisions we make. This is equally valid for all our decisions and activities, be they personal, in business, politics or any other sphere. These values can vary considerably among people within a culture and even more between people of different cultures.

When we begin to look more closely at values we begin to realize that all our thoughts, words and deeds are coloured by the values we hold in our heart. They operate at a very subtle level of our being such that we are not usually aware of how they influence and shape our perceptions and activities.

To obtain a better understanding of these vital influences, we shall first examine the nature of values and then consider the different types of values before engaging in a brief self-examination to consider what values we each hold dear.

Values are defined as principles or standards that guide our behaviour. We can have a number of standards that vie for priority. As discussed in the previous chapter, if one values material wealth as a measure of success, then one will act in order to obtain wealth. If one also values honesty sufficiently, then one would not lie in order to succeed. However, if honesty is not truly valued, if it is not a basis for one's decisions, then one would not hesitate to lie for the sake of financial gain.

Values are also defined as that which has intrinsic worth, goodness. To value something is to prize or esteem it. Something valued is important, it has priority. Something can be valued for its own sake, such as a friendship; or it can be valued as a means to bring about a better state, such as physical exercise to build a healthy body or the object of value can be the consequence or result, such as money.

For example, a salesperson whose primary value is money will be motivated to act in such a way as to maximize his sales commission. This often results in behaviour that may include saying whatever needs to be said to get the order. The prospect asks, 'Can you deliver by such a date? Will it include these non-standard features? Can I take 120 days to pay?'

We are all familiar with people who will answer 'yes' to all these questions regardless of whether it is acceptable, true or of benefit to their company. It is the expediency of the moment that matters.

Paul recalls:

> I began work as a sales representative directly after a four-year electrical engineering degree. I had no business experience but took a job selling large computer systems. I was assigned to a senior salesman who acted as my first mentor. This chap was lovable, but he came from a rich family and was not very motivated. He valued an easy life. One of my customers asked for a price quotation on a new piece of equipment that was not in the price book. When I asked my mentor's advice, he said, 'Just tell them it is the

same as the previous one. If it turns out to be different we will tell them later that it has changed.' I did as he bid.

Six months later I was reassigned to a very professional salesman for some additional training. The same situation occurred again; I was asked for a price quotation for which we had no information. Trying to impress my new mentor with my savvy, I suggested the same approach as used previously. He almost bit my head off. 'No you won't. You will call HQ and take whatever time it takes to find the answer. When you make a commitment to a customer, you make sure that you keep to it.' This was a very good lesson about integrity that has stayed with me these forty years.

In fact, I recently had to remind a young salesman in our company about the importance of keeping his word, about fulfilling his commitments.

While the temptation for the salesperson may be great to say just what he thinks the prospect wants to hear, those who value their personal honesty and their company's reputation more will answer in the affirmative only if the response is true and mutually beneficial for the company and the customer. This requires fine discrimination on the part of the sales person, which begins with holding the right values.

Chris's experience:

A salesman, who was very sharp but whom I had never trusted, came back from seeing a client, and reported to me proudly that he had just sold a big software contract. 'And the best thing about it' he said, 'is that we do not have to deliver anything.' Now I knew that no client ever paid a lot of money for a service which did not deliver anything, and as I had never trusted this salesman myself, I was very concerned. My concerns were justified: we ended up being sued by that client for non-performance.

Universal values

Values can be at different levels. Their scope can vary from the universal down to the individual. Universal values present a unified view. They relate to our essential nature and are applicable for all times, in all places and for everyone. Universal values relate to subjects such as love, justice and truth. In terms of their objectives they are concerned with the good of all, the common good.

One example of a universal principle setting out how we should act towards others is the so-called Golden Rule which has been expressed in various ways:

- Christian version: 'Do unto others as you would like them to do unto you' (Luke, 6:31); 'Love your neighbour as yourself' (Matthew 22:39);
- Hindu version: 'Let not any man do unto another any act that he wisheth not done to himself by others, knowing it to be painful to himself' (Shanti Parva, in *Mahabharata*, 1976 edn.);
- Confucian version: 'Do not do to others what you would not want them to do to you' (Confucius, *Analects*, 1971 edn.);
- Buddhist version: 'Hurt not others with that which pains yourself' (Udanavarga, undated);
- Jewish version: 'What is hateful to yourself do not do to your

fellow man. This is the whole Torah (Law).' (*Babylonian Talmud, Shabbath* (undated);

- Muslim version: 'No man is a true believer unless he desires for his brother that which he desires for himself. (*Hadith Muslim, imam 71–2* (undated).

The fact that all these traditions hold the same values, in strikingly similar words, is evidence that there are universal values which transcend different cultures, faiths, places and times.

Cultural values

Cultural values differ according to the language, laws and religion of a particular people. They also vary according to the time and place.

Cultural values have to do with the interpretation and application of universal values in various domains of life. They manifest as laws, social conventions and customs, and relate to issues such as economics, aesthetics, business ethics, and so on. These cultural values serve to maintain the social order. They become the basis for the body of ideas, opinions and beliefs of particular nations or cultural groups.

It is in these areas of life that the various cultural formulations apparently diverge considerably. For example, an aesthetic value may be seen in the type of music or art that is preferred (valued) in a society. This is usually different from the music or art valued in other cultures. The universal value of beauty is the same but what people call beautiful varies. Think of the differences in the music and art of China, India and the USA.

Cultural values are subtly absorbed into one's being through the influence of family, religion, the educational system, and increasingly television, radio and the newspapers. For example, a person raised in a European country with a university education will have been exposed to different cultural values from a person raised in India with only basic secondary education.

Chris writes:

> In the immediate aftermath of the demise of the Soviet Union I was in Russia, giving a series of seminars to officials from the Ministry of Privatization on how to undertake the task, based on our experience in the UK and Poland. At a reception I was asked by the Deputy Minister how my firm could help his Department. After discussing a number of possibilities, we agreed that he would send me their latest draft law on privatization and we would review it to assess how practicable it would be and identify any obstacles to its implementation. This was an excellent outcome and I promised to send him a proposal as soon as we returned to the UK. I sent him the proposal and then for some time heard nothing – not in itself very surprising. Imagine then my surprise when an official of the British Government Knowhow Fund, which had offered to assist with the cost, told me that a law firm, which had also participated in the seminars, had been asked to propose for the same work. There had been no sense of a competition for the work in my conversation with the Minister. I had never been informed that we were competing for the work. Was he being 'economical with the truth'? I concluded that the Russian approach to competition was just

culturally different from ours, where it is open and clear that a competition is taking place.

A year or so later, a major computer supplier that I was advising told me that they had secured a huge contract for PCs for a big Russian bank. I advised them to keep the champagne on ice. Having a contract with a Russian firm at that time was nice, but meant little. As I suspected, they had signed similar contracts with several other suppliers. What mattered was being on the ground, delivering equipment and getting paid for it – nothing else.

Did these experiences indicate that Russian businessmen were dishonest? There were certainly many examples of that, but in these instances it was more a case that the notion of a contract and the importance of contracts in business life were very new to them. It had not been at all significant under communism and it was not part of their culture.

Similarly one can consider the current business climate in Russia. There may be something in the cultural values of the country that has made it more susceptible to bribery than other countries. A recent study by a Russian research group in Moscow estimates that more than $300 billion in bribes is paid every year, two and a half times as much as the government collects in budget revenues. As one might expect, this corruption is a real obstacle to external investment in the country (Myers, 2005).

It is not inevitable that essential business values will differ between countries. In fact our findings seem to indicate that there is considerable common ground. Here are two statements of business values coming from two separate cultures:

To buy and sell, yet never to forget God: this is the idea to follow so that hand and heart work harmoniously.

Abu Said, *Rubaiyat*, 1992

Profit is a regulator in the life of a business, but it is not the only one. Other human and moral factors must also be considered which, in the long term, are at least as important for the life of a business.

Pope John Paul II, *Memory and Identity*, 2005

Individual values

The third dimension to consider in assessing one's own value system is the set of values that one has adopted. People raised in the same country, with the same religion and having the same education may have different sets of personal values due to varying temperaments and experiences. Individual values are:

● acquired through a combination of nature and nurture;

● subjective, based on personal experience;

● reflected in individual goals, commitments, preferences, priorities.

The obvious trend in the West over the last three to four hundred years has been more and more towards the democratic ideals of freedom and equality. However, there are still the vestiges of class distinction that cause people to acquire varying life values. Instead of heredity as the measure of class, money has now become the main differentiator. If, for example, one is born into a wealthy family, then one is more likely to live in an attractive and safe area, to get the opportunity for holidays abroad that open one's eyes to other cultures and to be educated in good schools. These experiences will affect one's values.

Those in the West not nurtured in this environment of the materially wealthy still have many opportunities available to them to grow and succeed. In fact, there are many examples where the lack of material riches has acted as a real stimulant for people to work very hard at succeeding. This experience generates another set of values.

Apart from the different environments in which people are raised, there are the evident pressures for individual rights. People today are encouraged to think for themselves, to form their own opinions and to be independent. In some companies this direction is reflected in a company policy which states that each employee is responsible for their own self-development. The company will help but it really is up to individual employees to look after themselves. This apparent freedom for the individual however carries with it the risk that it allows the employer to abdicate their responsibilities for the development of their staff.

With this focus on individual thought and initiative, it is no wonder that there is greater emphasis on personal opinion based on one's personal experience. This also means that the guidance offered from the pulpit on Sunday mornings is often taken as just another opinion and not necessarily better than one's own.

The plethora of individual opinions and beliefs has inevitably led to a very diverse melange of individual values within the framework of a culture. Even the more group-oriented cultures like China, Japan and India are finding it difficult to obtain full consensus on values. Access in these countries to the internet and to media from other cultures is awakening a desire for greater freedom of expression which inevitably leads to a wider range of individual values.

Spiritual values: what do you value in life?

The following is a summary of traditional values compiled from eight spiritual traditions: Buddhist, Christian, Greek, Islamic, Judaic, Sikh, Taoist and Vedic. It is a strikingly long list, but one that we have selected from the range of virtues advocated by these traditions (Armstrong, 2005). It gives ample scope for thought and practice.

Please spend a few moments considering this list, adding any others that come to mind. Then list the five values that are most important to you; the ones that guide your personal behaviour and decisions.

Benevolence	Gentleness	Pilgrimage
Charity	Harmlessness	Prudence
Compassion	Harmony	Harmony
Courage	Hope	Respect
Dignity	Hospitality	Righteousness
Equanimity	Humility	Self-Control
Faith	Integrity	Service
Fearlessness	Justice	Sincerity
Forgiveness	Lawfulness	Steadfastness
Perseverance	Love/Charity	Temperance
Freedom	Loyalty	Tolerance
Friendship	Obedience	Truthfulness
Generosity	Patience	Wisdom

Here is another set of values that might also be familiar to you. These are not however recommended by the spiritual teachers as the basis for our thoughts, words or deeds.

Material wealth   Physical beauty   Physical pleasure
Physical strength   Fame   Power

Look at the list of the five values that you have chosen. What were the factors that influenced you to make that selection? You may find that you chose them because something within you says that they are right and true. It may be that your religious upbringing influenced you to establish that value from your youth. It may also be that your experiences in life have demonstrated the importance of certain values in bringing happiness to yourself and others.

Here are two perspectives on this choice, one ancient, the other modern:

> Youth, beauty, life, riches, health, friends are things that pass, let not the wise man attach himself at all to these.
>
> *Mahabharata*, 1976 edn.
>
> If any man seeks for greatness, let him forget greatness and ask for truth, and he will find both.
>
> Horace Mann, cit. in *Thoughts on the Business of Life*, 1968

The question of values can be examined from a slightly different perspective.

If you were to start a company today, what are the five fundamental values of the organization that you would adopt?

Are they different from your selection of personal values? If so, why are they different?

Please keep this list for future reference. When you have finished the book, consider whether your list should change.

The area that we will now consider in some depth is that of moral values. Before proceeding to the next chapter, however, consider first for a moment your understanding of morality.

CHAPTER 3 - MORALITY AND VIRTUE

T he word moral comes from the Latin *mos* (pl. *mores*) meaning manner, customs, way of life, conduct or character. Morality is concerned with the way of life we choose and includes the distinctions between right and wrong, good and bad, the regulation of conduct and our responsibilities to others. Moral decisions are based on knowing right from wrong and acting correctly based on that knowledge. Decisions and actions that are opposed to or not conforming to morality, either because of a lack of the right knowledge or due to an unwillingness to act rightly, may be considered as immoral.

Moral principles relate to the meaning and purpose of our human existence. They also provide the foundation upon which our civil laws and business activities should be based. We all abide by what we individually consider to be moral, but there does not seem to be a general agreement as to what is moral. Here is one view.

> The noblest moral law is that we should unremittingly work
> for the good of mankind.

Mahatma Gandhi, cit. in *Indian Wisdom*, 2003

The reason that there is great disagreement about the decisions relating to right and wrong is that the prevailing attitude of a culture varies over time. What follows are descriptions of attitudes that influence our individual view as to the correctness of a decision. We call this the 'moral hierarchy' in that there appears to be a graded order whereby morality begins as the most important factor in a decision but it is then replaced, step by step, by expediency and personal opinion with little or no regard for morality. Some representative quotations have been added to help reinforce or clarify the meaning.

The Moral Hierarchy

Starting at the highest level:

1. WORK IS A SACRED ACTIVITY AND MUST BE PERFORMED FOR THE SAKE OF ALL.

Everything comes from God, thus everything is sacred; so there is no difference between the sacred and the profane.

> When one values and respects something as sacred, the best comes forth.
>
> St Benedict, *The Rule of St Benedict*, 1997 trans.

2. ACTIONS ARE FULLY GUIDED BY FAITH IN ONE'S SPIRITUAL/RELIGIOUS TEACHING. THERE IS OBEDIENCE TO ITS COMMANDMENTS.

> Thou shalt not bear false witness against thy neighbour.
>
> *Exodus* 20:12

3. ONE ACTS FROM A STRONG SENSE OF DUTY - DOING WHAT SHOULD BE DONE FOR HONOUR'S SAKE.

> My word is my bond
>
> Motto of the London Stock Exchange

4. DECISIONS ARE MADE BASED ON A UTILITARIAN VIEW, I.E. ONE IS GOOD BECAUSE IT PAYS TO BE GOOD, ALSO KNOWN AS ENLIGHTENED SELF-INTEREST.

Utilitarianism defines the chief consideration of morality as the greatest good or happiness of the greatest number. Thus the morality of any action or law is defined by its utility, i.e. the consequences of the action. Motive and intention are not important, it is the results that count.

5. ONE ACTS IN SUCH A WAY AS NOT TO VIOLATE THE RIGHTS OF OTHERS.

This is the beginning of a morality based on a contract, a social contract which is part of the fabric of the society. It can be a Bill of Rights (USA) or a Charter of Human Rights (European Union) designed to protect members of the community.

6. ONE ACTS BASED ON AN ESTABLISHED CODE OF PRACTICE OR STANDARD.

This may take the form of a code of conduct set by a government regulator, an industry association or a professional body, for example, the Financial Services Authority (FSA) in the UK; the Securities and Exchange Commission (SEC) in the USA, the Law Society, the Institute of Chartered Accountants in England and Wales.

7. THE BASIS FOR MORALITY IS WHETHER THE ACTION IS LEGAL, I.E. WHETHER IT VIOLATES THE WRITTEN LAWS OF THE LAND.

As long as an action is legal, it is permissible. Morality is not the issue. One can see that at this level the number of people employed in the legal departments of companies rises considerably.

8. MORALITY IS BASED ON MY JUDGEMENT, MY PERSONAL VIEW AS TO WHAT IS RIGHT OR GOOD.

When the written laws on an issue are unclear or open to a wide range of interpretations or when respect for the established authority diminishes substantially or when morality is deemed not to be important in a society, then an individual makes their own personal judgements.

At this level the watchwords of a democracy, freedom and equality, are taken to mean, 'I can do anything I want, it is my right; and all opinions are equally valid; my view is as good as yours, as good the view of the Church or of the state.'

What would you say are the dominant influences at play today? Which levels of the moral hierarchy seem to be operating?

Do we not hear a great deal today about rights, but very little about duties? (LEVEL 5)

Do not even the most altruistic of companies explain their policies and actions in terms of how doing good helps the bottom line? (LEVEL 4)

There have recently been a number of pleas from business leaders for governments and the European Commission to slow the pace of introducing new corporate governance legislation as companies risk being snowed under by new laws (LEVEL 6) (*Accountancy Age*, 2005).

How often nowadays do you hear explicitly or implicitly, 'My word is my bond?' 'I have made a commitment, and I shall honour it, no matter how expensive or inconvenient.' (LEVEL 3)

Have you heard the Bible quoted recently when a business decision was being considered? (LEVEL 2)

Consider your own experience of the decision-making criteria typically used in meetings you have attended. Quite commonly we ask

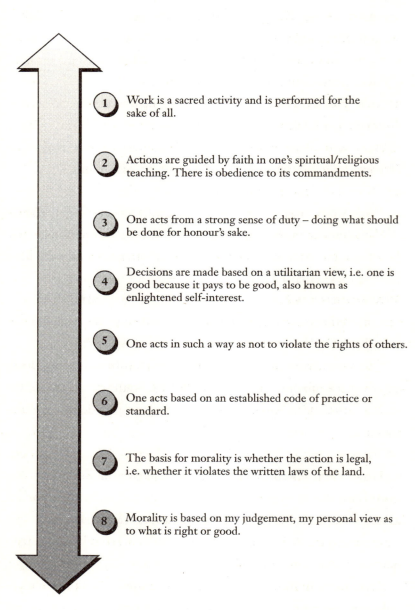

1. Work is a sacred activity and is performed for the sake of all.

2. Actions are guided by faith in one's spiritual/religious teaching. There is obedience to its commandments.

3. One acts from a strong sense of duty – doing what should be done for honour's sake.

4. Decisions are made based on a utilitarian view, i.e. one is good because it pays to be good, also known as enlightened self-interest.

5. One acts in such a way as not to violate the rights of others.

6. One acts based on an established code of practice or standard.

7. The basis for morality is whether the action is legal, i.e. whether it violates the written laws of the land.

8. Morality is based on my judgement, my personal view as to what is right or good.

such questions as, 'Will this decision produce the most profit? Will it help reduce costs? Will it please the boss? Will it solve the immediate problem?' How many times has the question been raised, '*Is this right?*'

Given these influences, is it a surprise that those who advocate moral principles as the basis for decisions are in the minority? However, David Pitt-Watson, Chief Executive of Hermes Focus Asset Management, addressing a DTI conference in London in December 2005, advocated moving up the moral hierarchy. He said, 'We can't legislate from Brussels and we probably can't legislate from a national government. We need soft laws, professional standards, understandings. We need owners to take responsibility. We need ethics and agreement on goals.' (*Accountancy Age*, 2005)

Why be moral?

A question that often arises in societies where religious tradition has been separated from secular activities is, 'Why be moral?'

The response to this begins with other questions. Why is it universally acknowledged that we should treat others as we would be treated, the Golden Rule? Could it be because others are not fundamentally different from oneself?

There are clearly many physical differences between people including body, language and gene patterns. But in another sense people are the same throughout the world. Sorrow, fear, faith, hope, desire, happiness, all transcend geographical, national and denominational differences. The mental and emotional instruments, i.e. the mind and the heart, are essentially the same in all men and women; however, they have been used in particular ways such that no two individuals anywhere think, speak or act in exactly the same way. This differentiation of the various physical and subtle forms of mankind explains how different cultural and individual values flow naturally from the universal principles. However, what needs to be remembered is that the underlying unity is the basis for morality.

> The infinite oneness of the Soul is the eternal sanction of all morality. You and I are not only brothers, but you and I are really one.
>
> This oneness is the rationale of all ethics.
>
> Swami Vivekananda, cit. in *Indian Wisdom*, 2003

The foundation of trust is therefore the simple recognition that we are essentially not different or separate. Immorality springs from a sense of separateness and division.

This perspective means that enlightened selfishness, where one subscribes to moral rules and precepts from clever calculation of the balance of one's gains over losses, is not a true basis for morality.

There is little doubt that adherence to personal and social morality promotes the well-being of a society. It helps in the maintenance of law and order, social cohesion, respect for the way of life of others and personal integrity. In today's difficult business environment, behaviour based on such values is indisputably finer, but if challenging circumstances arise one can be easily knocked off balance.

When the basis for morality is linked with unchanging, intrinsic universal principles, then it operates as a preparatory discipline for true self-understanding and true happiness for all. It is part of something greater rather than an end in itself. Hence the importance of such fundamental questions as 'What is the best kind of life?', and 'How should we live?'. These are questions that the great teachers, like Plato, Moses and Confucius, have encouraged their followers to ask themselves. They then guided them to the realization that living a virtuous life is the key to happiness for all.

Virtue

What then is a virtuous life and how does such a life relate to being an effective manager?

> It was about this time that I conceived the bold and arduous Project of arriving at Moral Perfection. I wished to live without committing any Fault at any time; I would conquer all that either Natural Inclination, Custom, or Company might lead me into. As I knew, or thought I knew, what was right and wrong, I did not see why I might not always do the one and avoid the other. But I soon found I had undertaken a Task of more Difficulty than I had imagined. While my Attention was taken up guarding against one Fault, I was often surprised by another. Habit took the Advantage of Inattention. Inclination was sometimes too strong for Reason. I concluded at length, that the mere speculative Conviction that it was our Interest to be completely virtuous, was not sufficient to prevent our slipping, and that the contrary Habits must be broken, and good ones acquired and established, before we can have any Dependence on a steady uniform Rectitude of conduct.
>
> Benjamin Franklin, *The Art of Virtue*, 1996 edn.

When moral principles are lived, that is, put into practice fully, this demonstrates virtue. People who behave in this way are called virtuous. Many of the great philosophers and spiritual teachers have claimed that a human being's greatest happiness comes from living a virtuous life, a life true to one's nature. Confucius and Plato were remarkably alike in their teaching about virtue as a source of true efficiency and happiness. They also agreed that acting virtuously required that one had knowledge about virtue and that this knowledge could be taught.

> If we observe we shall find that all human virtues increase
> and strengthen themselves by the practice and experience of
> them.
>
> Plato, *Laws*
>
> The gentleman (ideal man) is not invariably for or against
> anything. He is on the side of what is moral.
>
> Confucius, *Analects*, 1971 edn.

It is valuable to examine the nature of virtue using the words of respected teachers from various cultures as our guide. Virtue is defined as moral excellence, uprightness, goodness. Plato spoke of virtue as the common property of all. He said that virtue is to delight in things honourable and to have the power of getting them justly.

> To be virtuous is to bring harmony to the soul.
>
> Plato, *Laws*

While emphasis is placed on different virtues by different cultures, there is general agreement on the nature of a virtuous person. These virtues actually describe the true dignity of a human being, the full potential. It is the model to which we can all aspire as it is a description of our true nature. It is common to all people, in all places, at all times.

> In observing the commandments we come to discover the virtues. In observing the commandment not to lie, we come to learn about the virtue of truthfulness and its positive natural aspects.
>
> Pope John Paul II, *Memory and Identity*, 2005

In ancient China the terms of an agreement were inscribed on a wooden tablet, the debit or obligations being on the left and the credit or dues on the right. It was then broken in two and each of the contracting parties kept his own half until fulfilment was demanded, when the validity of the claim was tested by fitting the two halves together.

> The virtuous person having entered into an agreement adheres to his obligations (literally: he holds to the left side of the agreement) but does not exact fulfilment from others. He attends to the spirit of the compact; while the man without virtue attends only to the claims.
>
> Lao Tse, *Sayings of Lao Tse*, 1976 edn.

Here is a list of virtues, again gleaned from various spiritual traditions, together with a representative quotation. The difference between values and virtues is that virtues are the finest values put into practice, lived, made natural. It is by practice under all conditions that virtue becomes established.

Wisdom

Wisdom is the foundation of virtue. It embodies both knowledge and the state of one's being. To be wise is to put the knowledge into practice.

Wisdom is like unto a beacon set on high, which radiates its
light even in the darkest night.

Japanese Buddhist Meditation, cit. in Mencken, 1946

Patience

Patience is an aspect of constancy. One holds firm, is steadfast and
resolved. To be patient means learning to wait for the right moment
to act.

If you do not cover yourself on every side with the shield of
patience, you will not long remain without wounds.

Thomas À Kempis, *The Imitation of Christ*, 1995 edn.

Self-Control

There is much unhappiness, stress and conflict in the world because of
failure to control tempers, appetites, passions and impulses. Plato
divided the Soul into three parts: reason, passion and appetite and said
that right behaviour results from harmony or control of these elements.

Should not all men hold self-control to be the foundation of
all virtue and first establish this firmly in their souls?

Plato, *Republic*

Courage

Courage is often defined as bravery or fearlessness, but to be truly
courageous (and not reckless) means feeling appropriate degrees of
fear and confidence in challenging situations.

Holding fast to one's own roots is the foundation of courage.

To see what is right and not to do it is cowardice.

Confucius, *Analects*, 1971 edn.

Justice

Justice is that cardinal virtue that is best described as giving to each what is due. Essential to justice is the concept of fairness.

> I believe that justice is instinct and innate, that the moral
> sense is as much a part of our constitution as that of feeling,
> seeing and hearing.

Thomas Jefferson, cit. in *The Portable Thomas Jefferson*

Faith

Faith is the source of discipline and power. It is a potent force in human experience, one which binds people together in a unique way.

> Nothing so cements and holds together all the parts of a
> society as faith or credit, which can never be kept up unless
> men are under some force or necessity of honestly paying
> what they owe to one another.

Cicero, 1971 edn.

Perseverance

Perseverance means continuing steadfastly in the pursuit of an aim. It means overcoming hesitation, vacillating, and the desire to quit. It can act for good if accompanied by practical intelligence.

> God helps those who persevere.

The Qu'ran

Charity

Charity is love for humanity and includes the kindness, affection and support one happily gives to another.

> Let all your things be done with Charity.

1 *Corinthians*

Forgiveness

To forgive is to let go, to cease to resent, to pardon. It brings freedom for all.

To err is human, to forgive is divine.

Alexander Pope, *An Essay on Criticism*, 2004 edn.

Forgive us our trespasses as we forgive those who trespass against us.

The Lord's Prayer

Temperance

Temperance is getting the balance right: everything in its proper measure. It requires moderation and self-restraint.

One must know how to choose the mean and avoid the extremes on either side as far as possible.

Aristotle, *Nicomachean Ethics*, 1995 edn.

Whoever cultivates the golden mean avoids the poverty of the hovel and the envy of the palace.

Horace, *Odes*, 1994 edn.

Truthfulness/Honesty

Honesty expresses both self-respect and respect for others.

This above all,

To thine own self be true;

And it shall follow as the night the day,

Thou canst not then be false to any man.

Shakespeare, *Hamlet*

Generosity

To be generous is to be magnanimous (*magnus*, great, *animus*, mind), noble minded and never mean or prejudiced.

> The quickest generosity is the best.
>
> Arab proverb, cit. in Mencken, 1946

Dignity

Dignity signifies worth, excellence, honour and natural stateliness.

> The real dignity of a man lies not in what he has, but what he is.
>
> John Stuart Blackie, *On Self-culture*, 1882

Tolerance

A tolerant person endures, permits, allows others the freedom to exist without interference.

> People were created for the sake of one another. Either teach them or bear with them.
>
> Marcus Aurelius, *Spiritual Teachings*, 1967 edn.

Humility

Humility is often misunderstood as weakness. In fact, it is indicative of great strength; it enables one to learn and is the very antithesis of pride.

> The fruits of humility are love and peace.
>
> Hebrew proverb, cit. in Mencken

Non-violence

Violence is doing harm, physical, mental or emotional, to another.

The extension of the law of non-violence to the domain of
economics means nothing less than the introduction of
moral values as a factor to be considered in regulating international commerce.

Mahatma Gandhi, cit. in *Indian Wisdom*, 2003

Absence of anger

Anger, which often leads to violence, manifests when a desire is
frustrated. The stronger the desire, the more violent the reaction.

When you are angry, be assured that it is not only a present
evil, but that you have increased an evil.

Epictetus, *The Art of Living*, 1995 edn.

Compassion

Compassion is the active disposition towards fellowship and sharing, towards supportive companionship when another is in dis-
tress.

Be ye all of one mind, having compassion one of another.

St Paul, *Epistle to Peter*, 3:8

Hope

Hope as a virtue is a feeling of great trust and promise.

So long as I breathe I have hope (*Dum spiro, spero*).

Roman proverb, cit. in Mencken 1946 edn.

Equanimity

Equanimity is maintaining the balance between apparent opposites such that the opposing forces are no longer seen as antagonistic but simply different expressions of the same subject.

> Make pain and pleasure, loss and gain, victory and defeat equal to you, then turn yourself to battle, and so you shall have no sin.
>
> *Bhagavad Gita*, 1977 trans

Steadfastness

Constant, firm, unwavering, free.

> When you have seen your aim, hold to it, firm and unshakeable.
>
> *Dhammapada*, 1973 edn.

Love

Love is unity; it is when two become one.

> An atom of love is to be preferred to all that exists between the two horizons.
>
> Farid-uddin Attar, cit. in *Eternal Wisdom*, 1995

Freedom

Freedom at its finest is having no dependence on anything external to one's self while still acknowledging one's commonality with all. With freedom comes responsibility.

> Freedom is for Love. It is given to man as a task to be accomplished. There is no freedom without truth.
>
> Pope John Paul II, *In My Own Words*, 2005

Obedience

True obedience is compliance with the law governing any task or duty. It involves the surrender of one's own will for the sake of the work.

> He who has not learned to obey cannot be a good
> commander.
>
> Aristotle

Hospitality

Hospitality indicates a friendly and generous reception of guests, be they friends or strangers. It represents openness.

> Hospitality is even to be shown to the enemy. The tree does
> not withdraw its shade even from the woodcutter.
>
> *Hitopadesa* - Indian spiritual text, cit. in *Eternal Wisdom*

Friendship

The demands of friendship are for honesty, for self-revelation, for taking one's friend's criticisms as seriously as their expression of admiration or praise, for loyalty, for unselfish support. Friendship brings out the best in the other.

> There can be no friendship where there is no freedom.
> Friendship loves the free air and will not be fenced up in
> straight and narrow enclosures.
>
> William Penn, *The Fruits of Solitude*, 1978 edn.

Respect

Respect is the esteem or honour in which we hold our fellow human beings. With respect we treat them with consideration and refrain from harming them.

> Respect man as a spiritual being in whom dwells the Divine
> Spirit.
>
> Leo Tolstoy, cit. in *Eternal Wisdom*

> Let us respect men and not only men of worth, but the pub-
> lic in general.
>
> Cicero

Sincerity

Sincerity means freedom from pretence or deceit. There is then no
difference between the reality and the appearance.

> Sincerity, a profound, grand, ingenuous sincerity is the first
> characteristic of all men who are in any way heroic.
>
> Thomas Carlyle, *On Heroes, Hero-Worship and Heroes in History*, 1966 edn.

An exercise in recognizing virtues

As an exercise in recognizing the presence of these virtues, please
read the following poem, *IF* by Rudyard Kipling. The theme of this
poem is virtue and the true dignity of man. Read the poem through
fully and then read the lines indicated pausing after each to consider
which of the virtues are being described.

If

> If you can keep your head when all about you
> Are losing theirs and blaming it on you, (1)
> If you can trust yourself when all men doubt you
> But make allowance for their doubting too, (2)

If you can wait and not be tired by waiting,   (3)

Or being lied about, don't deal in lies,   (4)

Or being hated, don't give way to hating,   (5)

And yet don't look too good, nor talk too wise:

If you can dream – and not make dreams your master,

If you can think – and not make thoughts your aim;

If you can meet with Triumph and Disaster

And treat those two impostors just the same;   (6)

If you can bear to hear the truth you've spoken

Twisted by knaves to make a trap for fools,   (7)

Or watch the things you gave your life to, broken,

And stoop and build 'em up with worn-out tools: (8)

If you can make one heap of all your winnings

And risk it all on one turn of pitch-and-toss,

And lose, and start again at your beginnings

And never breath a word about your loss;   (9)

If you can force your heart and nerve and sinew

To serve your turn long after they are gone,   (10)

And so hold on when there is nothing in you

Except the Will which says to them: 'Hold on!'   (11)

If you can talk with crowds and keep your virtue,   (12)

Or walk with kings – nor lose the common touch,   (13)

If neither foes nor loving friends can hurt you;

If all men count with you, but none too much,

If you can fill the unforgiving minute

With sixty seconds' worth of distance run,   (14)

Yours is the Earth and everything that's in it,

And—which is more – you'll be a Man, my son!

Consider how the virtues described in the poem would be applied in business. How would someone with these virtues manage him- or herself and how would they manage and lead others? Compare your answers with our view below:

(1) Steadfastness

(2) Forgiveness

(3) Patience

(4) Truthfulness

(5) Absence of Anger

(6) Equanimity

(7) Tolerance

(8) Perseverance

(9) Non-Attachment

(10) Self-Control

(11) Faith

(12) Integrity

(13) Humility

(14) Steadfastness

CHAPTER 4 - ADVOCATES OF THE

The religious and spiritual traditions have had great influence on the laws, ethics and moral values of their societies. This influence has been cyclical in that at times it has been more pronounced, more direct and more effective. At other times when the principles have been forgotten or ignored, the negative impact on society has been clearly observed.

The danger to global cooperation in the matter of morality has been described as religious 'egoism', that is, 'My view is better than yours'. It is necessary to look objectively at the main tenets of some of the main traditions, Eastern and Western, to assess whether there are more similarities than differences when it comes to the view on morality and virtue.

The Judaeo-Christian view

In the West the main influence on behaviour has been the Judaeo-Christian tradition, particularly the Bible and the teachings of Moses and Christ.

As described in Chapter One, the traditional view of the Christian Church towards money and affluence has changed dramatically over the years. It has shifted back and forth, from rejection of business as an unfit occupation for Christians to the other extreme where wealthy businessmen are honoured members of the community.

A current Christian view has been expounded in a recent report issued by the organization Churches Together in Britain and

MORAL WAY

Ireland, entitled *Prosperity with a Purpose: Christians and the Ethics of Affluence* (Churches Together, 2005). The paper is built upon the reports of other Christian church organizations:

- *The Common Good* (Catholic Bishops, 1996), which set forth a fundamental principle that market forces should be society's servants, not its masters.
- *Unemployment and Work* (Council of Churches, 1997) which attempted to dispel the myth that unemployment and the related human suffering were inevitable.

The key conclusion which emerged from the report is that under the right conditions, economic growth can serve God's purposes. The primary conditions are that wealth creation and the pursuit of social justice are inextricably linked and that market forces do encourage economic growth, but should be regulated when necessary in the interests of the community.

The report sets out principles described below that seem quite consistent with the values of other traditions.

- Every man and woman has the right to prosper but in addition, also has the responsibility to recognize that others have the same right.
- The ideal of a well-ordered society, where individual and social rights and responsibilities are in balance, will enable the overcoming of poverty, the creation and fair distribution of wealth and advances in human progress and development.
- Christians have to recognize that the creation of wealth by

economic activity is one of the chief engines of progress and greater wellbeing, and to thank God for it.

- The pursuit of profit as an end in itself frequently results in hardship and injustice. A market-based economy, given free rein, can increase both wealth and poverty. When market forces detract from the common good they need to be restrained.
- Most companies in the private sector are eager to conduct themselves as good corporate citizens and to be seen to do so.
- They know that the very possibility of engaging in commerce depends upon the existence of at least a minimum level of respect, trust and honesty. It is a matter of concern to business people as much as church people when society seems to be heading away from those minimum levels of trust and honesty.
- Christians have to be aware of the complexity and interdependence of the many factors involved. Moral principles applied simplistically and without due respect for economic analysis can easily lead to erroneous solutions.
- Churches need the input of those of their members who possess expertise in this field as well as the work of specialists in social ethics from the various religious traditions, past and present.
- While the key principles derived from the Christian faith are broadly unchanging, their application in particular circumstances must always be open for review.

In summary it is acceptable to be affluent as long as you play your role in creating a more just and sustainable society that serves the common good.

The Indian view

India has had both a strong spiritual tradition and a rich trading history. The products of India such as spices, precious stones and silk have been vital to Western trade for more than two thousand years.

Over the centuries in addition to the local Indian influence, both Muslim and Christian cultures have also left their traces, and helped form the values and moral attitudes of the country.

The native Vedic tradition of India, which goes back thousands of years, offers a very specific view of business. The role of the merchant class is to create wealth for the whole society. Wealth itself is instrumental, i.e. it is seen as a means to a finer and higher goal and not as an end in itself. The availability of sufficient wealth in a society enables the rulers to concentrate on their prime responsibilities to rule justly and the spiritual leaders to concentrate on the education and spiritual well-being of everyone.

While the Indian caste system which is the basis for the differentiation of duties in society has become rigid and corrupted, its original aim was to promote the unity and solidarity of the society. The key to understanding the system is the premise that there are four fundamental functions that must be performed to sustain the strength and well-being of any society. These are the spiritual and educational function, the ruling/political/military function, the merchant function which also includes artisans, and the function of manual work. When these are performed by specialists in harmony, the society will operate at its full potential for the benefit of all.

One of the earliest guides to the merchant class comes from the ancient legal treatise, the *Laws of Manu*.

Let him exert himself to the utmost in order to increase his

prosperity in a righteous manner and let him zealously give
food to all created beings.

Laws of Manu, ix (1979 edn.)

One of the most formative influences for many Indians has been
the *Bhagavad Gita*, meaning the Song of God, which is part of the
longest epic poem in existence, the *Mahabharata*. In the *Bhagavad
Gita*, Sri Krishna, a divine embodiment, gives advice to a great war-
rior, Arjuna. There are many passages that can be applied to business and management, but one of the most relevant to our
discussion of virtues and values is taken from a section where the
godly qualities are being described. One of these qualities is purity
of heart which means, according to Adi Sankara, who lived about
the ninth century and is regarded as the greatest commentator on
the text, 'abandonment of deception, dissimulation, falsehood and
the like in all transactions: that is to say, transacting business in perfect honesty'.

Even though the twentieth century was not a period of great
economic success for the Indian people, during this period it
became the largest democracy in the world and is now poised to
begin fulfilling its potential as a global economic power. The Indian
people have had continual reminders during this period from wise
men who have offered excellent advice and guidance as to the values and morality of life.

> It is this desire to express himself that leads a man to search
> for riches and power. But he must understand that to accu-
> mulate wealth is not to find this fulfilment. What brings him
> back to himself is the inner light and not external objects.
>
> Rabindranath Tagore, in *Indian Wisdom*, 2003

A well known advocate of the moral way who lived and died for his values was Mahatma Gandhi. He had much to say on the subject including this:

> True morality consists not in following the well-beaten track, but in finding out the true path for ourselves and in fearlessly following it.
>
> Mahatma Gandhi, in *Indian Wisdom*, 2003

It will become increasingly important if one wants to do business in India to appreciate how the great spiritual heritage of this nation continues to influence the values and mores of the people.

The Chinese view

With a culture that goes back more than 5000 years the Chinese still remain an enigma to much of the West. The isolation of China from the West up until relatively modern times and the fact that for the last two hundred years the Chinese culture has been at a low ebb in its cycle have caused many people, as recently as 15 years ago, to discount China as a backward, developing country. The lengthy period during the twentieth century when the nation was under communist domination further clouded the view of the West. Yet when one begins to examine their history, their culture, their spiritual traditions and their economic prowess as demonstrated over the last 2500 years, it becomes clear that China has re-established its place as a major influence and power. Business people are already hard at work attempting to learn more about the Chinese cultural values as they relate to business.

Here is one very brief comparative assessment of some British versus Chinese values (International Communications Training Institute, 2004):

British values	Chinese values
Respect for law	Respect for family/state
Diplomacy/negotiations	Personal contacts
Individual freedom	Group stability
The contract	Friendship
Punctuality	Time is relative

Confucius, one of the major influences on Chinese values, developed a teaching that, upon his death, was promulgated throughout China by his 70 major disciples and then later through the writings of Mencius and his followers. Confucius took an educational approach to lead people to a good life. As noted in Chapter Three, he based his teaching on the belief that with knowledge man would act virtuously and that virtue inevitably brought the lasting happiness we all seek. He developed an image of the true gentlemen, the superior person:

> In his private conduct he was humble, in serving his superiors he was respectful, in nourishing the people he was kind and in ordering the people he was just.
>
> Confucius, *Analects*, 1971 edn.

An eloquent description of the qualities of a moral manager!

The influence of Buddhism has also been an important factor in the formulation of Chinese values. This teaching, which originated in India, spread to Korea and Japan and was instrumental in the cultural development of those countries as well.

The Buddha recommended an eight-fold path as a guide for life. It may be divided into three distinct areas that were of particular concern to the Buddha; wisdom, morality and meditation. The second area, morality, is the most relevant for our considerations.

Morality involves speech, action and the way we gain our livelihood.

Right Speech concerns the truth, holding the words of truth in mind, and speaking from that truth in a way that is true.

Right Action is a direct result of refined ideas. If our thoughts and words are of the nature of greed, hatred and delusion then our actions must be likewise. How different are actions that arise out of their opposites: generosity, compassion and understanding.

Right Livelihood is a way of sustaining ourselves which minimizes the impact we have on others and the world in general. In gaining our living we may feel that circumstances force us into ignoring such considerations, but Right Livelihood encourages to think differently, to appreciate the interconnectedness of all things and to tread lightly with due care and compassion.

William Wray, *Sayings of the Buddha*, 2005

The communist era has left its mark on China's business processes and its current views on ethics. In a culture where all is supposedly owned collectively by everyone, certain assumptions can arise that are in direct conflict with Western views on issues such as intellectual property.

The Chinese are already busy trying to master the ways of

Western business and are making very good progress. Their grow-ing dominance in the manufacturing of all types of products from clothing to computers is now being recognized as a potential threat to the manufacturing industries of many countries. This rapid progress is indicative of the future economic importance of China and the need to understand its business values.

A friend told us of his experience of learning the Confucian way:

'When I joined a large pharmaceutical organization as a cor-porate planner I was told that most of the staff in the nations for which I would be responsible had little or no concept of corporate loyalty and we had to earn it. They understood loyalty to the family, to a tribe or to an individ-ual, but not to an abstract like the company or the state. Most of what we call nepotism or corruption is merely ful-filling normal family obligations. Therefore if any of our expatriate managers was really effective with the local politicians and staff I was to recognize that expressions of goodwill to the company were to him, not us. I had to earn similar personal respect before anything said to me was more than mere politeness, telling the man from head office what he wants to hear.

'Our senior Far Eastern accountant, who was himself part of the elite which ran Singapore, educated me in the Confucian view of morality – as part of a very polite way of working out my price before equally politely agreeing how I would help ensure that we would be a good corporate citi-zen in return for his full co-operation in meeting our corpo-rate objectives. A key point was that the price can be pride,

family loyalty, ambition, etc., not just money. His first loyalty was to Singapore, not us, and his price was our good
citizenship. He also had a strong puritan morality which
coincided with mine but we were too polite to delve into
such personal matters as faith.'

The Japanese view

Japan, like China, is a very ancient culture with a very strong work
ethic. It grew at a terrific rate in the 1970s and 1980s to become the
second largest economic power in the world today. This achieve-
ment is even more significant when one considers that Japan is an
island nation with a dearth of natural resources. The intensity and
energy of the Japanese are reminiscent of the accomplishments of
another island nation, Great Britain, 150 years earlier.

After several years in recession, the Japanese appear again to be
building up an economic strength that makes them a strong candi-
date to be a leader in the global business community. It is important
to understand the cultural nuances that have gone into the establishment of their system of business mores, which in many ways are
similar to those of China.

The Japanese adapted many of their beliefs and philosophy from
the eighth-century T'ang Dynasty of China, when Buddhism was
the dominating influence. The qualities of Buddhism described
above were very important in the formulation of the principles of
Japanese morality.

In the seventeenth century Jocho Yamamoto, a samurai turned
priest, set out a system of ethics in an influential work called
Hagakure. His rules and principles for the samurai have been

adapted for use in business and other activities of Japanese life.

In Book One of the *Hagakure*, Yamamoto wrote:

> A calculating man is a coward because calculations are to do
> with profit and loss and such a person is therefore constantly
> preoccupied with profit and loss only.
>
> Jocho Yamamoto, *Hagakure*, 2000 edn.

This is not to say that profits and success are not to be sought but that they should not be the basis for one's actions.

Prior to the nineteenth century, Japan had a thriving business culture dominated by merchant houses. The oldest of these, Mitsui, is said to have been founded in 1632. These houses were owned and managed by members of large clans with their management ranks supplemented by trained professional managers, called *banto*, who were recruited from the lower social classes. They became a class of professional business managers.

Their trade was almost entirely confined within the Japanese market. Japan and China were in fact isolated from the western world for almost 300 years until the arrival of aggressive traders from the USA and Europe in the 1850s.

Yukichi Fukuzawa, a political economist and teacher, was instrumental in the assimilation of Japan into the world markets. He founded a university at Keio in 1858 and taught there, urging young Japanese people to take up careers in business and politics. He often stated that the ideal Japanese businessman would have the virtues of a samurai: dedication, honour, perseverance, loyalty and care for others.

Following him was Eiichi Shibusawa who felt that Japan should adopt Western business and management forms but at the same time retaining that which was best in the Japanese culture. He believed that private interests were identical to public ones and that it was in the public interest to increase national wealth. He spoke often of the duties of the businessman to his country.

The policies that emerged from this period had a lasting influence on the development of the Japanese economy into the twentieth century. As in many other aspects of life, the Japanese have been very adroit at extracting what is good and useful from other business systems while retaining a Japanese foundation. A strong emphasis on business education was one of their fundamental policies. While it necessarily focused on technical knowledge, it also included general knowledge about Western cultures. Western philosophy, art and literature were also studied, analysed and dissected in the search for any ideas that might be useful. Their attitude, which holds a good lesson for Western business, was to learn from your competitors and be willing to change so as to become, not like them, but better than them.

Benevolence is another virtue greatly valued by the Japanese. The attitude of Japanese companies to their employees is indicative of the importance of this attribute. Until very recent times, the duty of care to employees meant that when someone was employed it was for life. While lay-offs have been necessary over the last five to ten years, there still remains a deep concern for the welfare of employees. Such commitments made to employees and also to shareholders are taken very seriously, highlighting the importance of responsibility and accountability. It has been observed that when adversity strikes a Japanese company it is the person in charge, the

CEO, who will stand up to apologize for the crisis and will often resign as a means of self punishment (Witzel, 2004).

The Islamic view

> A man's true wealth hereafter is the good he does in the world to his fellow-man. When he dies, people will say, 'What property has he left behind him?' But the angels will ask, 'What good deeds has he sent before him?'
>
> Muhammad

Islam actively encourages Muslims to be involved in business and commerce. When Allah's Messenger was asked what type of earning was best, he replied, 'A man's work with his hand and every business transaction which is approved' (Azmi, 2005).

To a Muslim a lawful, approved action (*halal*) is ethical and an unlawful activity (*haram*) is unethical. These are some of the basic principles pertaining to *halal* and *haram*:

- To make lawful and to prohibit is the right of Allah alone.
- The prohibition of things is due to their impurity and their harmfulness.
- Whatever is conducive to *haram* is itself *haram*.
- Good intentions do not make the *haram* acceptable.
- The *haram* is prohibited to everyone alike.

Here is a summary of the some of the main principles for Muslims in business:

- Love Allah more than your trade or business.
- Be honest and truthful.
- Keep your word.
- Be humble in how you conduct your life.

- Use mutual consideration in your affairs.
- Do not deal in fraud.
- Deal justly.

Islamic tradition also provides for the social responsibility of the organization, which has a duty to protect and contribute to the society in which it functions. This covers:

- Its employees and all those involved in the business;
- The environment;
- The general social welfare of the society, including the poor.

The importance of taking care of the weak is stressed in many passages (*hadith*) in Islamic scripture. For instance, if a person spends a night hungry, the blame is shared by the community because it did not attempt to take care of him. It is therefore the responsibility of any Muslim organization to contribute to charities (Klesc, 2005).

This is the experience of a Muslim businessman:

'My grandfather was a moral person and a very successful businessman. He truly lived the maxim, 'my word is my bond'. He never had to write down any agreement; a spoken commitment and a shake of hands sealed the bond. The example set by my grandfather, of someone who was highly principled yet eminently successful, made a strong impression on me.

'I must admit that I was not always able to resist the temptations of taking short cuts in the business process. In the business culture in which I have operated, the giving of gifts is a common practice, one which can easily lead to abuse. On one occasion I made an offer to a very high-ranking government official who politely refused on the grounds that it would not be fair or just for his people. This was not just an isolated response as I later learned. Here was a person who, for the sake of the people he served, was not moved by personal gain. Another good example for me.

'In another situation I found myself on the other side. For a few years my business purchased manufactured goods from a supplier. As technology changed and new competitors came into the field, it was clear to us that we were paying twenty-five per cent more than what was on offer in the market. I wanted to be loyal to my supplier but I needed a lower cost of supply.

'In our negotiations I made it clear that I favoured staying with them but that we would have to see a reduction in cost. They negotiated very hard and would not move much at all on the price. I was determined that we had to have a better price. On the last evening of my visit, attractive young ladies were sent to my hotel room, courtesy of the supplier. I did not allow them in.

'The next day when I was supposed to meet the supplier for a final meeting, another man showed up with a package for me containing £100,000 as a gift in order to secure my agreement. I turned it down and left shortly thereafter.

'We signed a deal with another supplier within weeks at a price twenty-three per cent less than we had been paying, for products that were of higher quality.'

Conclusion

The Parliament of World Religions, a meeting of leaders from all the major religions, met first in 1893 and most recently in 2004. At its 1999 meeting all the leaders present agreed that religion has the power and the obligation to provide leadership in the realm of establishing an agreed system of global ethics. They agreed too that all religions share common moral principles, which were summarized as follows (Parliament of World Religions, 1999):

- **Truthfulness** – knowing the truth and expressing it fully. As one thinks, so one speaks and thus one acts.
- **Love/Benevolence** – as exemplified in the principle, "Love thy neighbour as thyself".
- **Justice** – to give each their due.
- **Freedom** – renouncing all that binds us, which prevents us from manifesting all the possibilities offered by our humanity.

In the following chapters we explore some practical ways in which these fine principles can become a reality in our business activities. Chapters Six to Eight will explore ways in which these universal principles can be made manifest; subsequent chapters examine the conditions in a company that would follow in terms of finer, more inclusive service, creativity, more productive individuals and more inspiring leadership.

CHAPTER 5 - PRINCIPLES: THE

What needs to be considered is not only the nature of these universal principles, but also whether they are truly understood, or interpreted in the light of current opinion or fashion. As a manager you need to understand the source and substance of your company's values and, assuming that you agree with them, live them and encourage your staff to do the same.

One view is that a company is a machine for making money, i.e. labour, capital and resources *in* and profit *out*. If that is the case then its values will be mechanistic, concerned with tools, processes and financial outputs.

If on the other hand your company is considered to be a living entity made up of people joined together in a common aim, then the values will more likely be concerned with issues such as morality, creativity and fulfilling potential.

In the USA, where the debate on the nature and purpose of companies has been going on now for more than a century, Professor William Allen from New York University's Stern School of Business calls these two ideas 'the property conception' and the 'social entity conception'. The first sees the company's aim as being to advance the financial interests of the owners. The second views the company as having a duty of loyalty to all those with some interest in or affected by the company (Skapinker, 2005).

This latter view is the argument underlying the currently popular concept of corporate social responsibility (CSR) which actually goes back some time. At the end of the 19th century, Carnegie in the USA

FOUNDATION OF A BUSINESS

and Rowntree and Cadbury in the UK took their paternalistic responsibilities for their workers and the neighbourhood seriously. To a large extent their values were based on two principles:

1. the 'charity principle' which held that one should assist the less fortunate such as the elderly, handicapped, sick and the unemployed (the deserving poor);

2. the 'stewardship principle' which requires that business organizations should act as caretakers of the land and people and hold these in trust for the benefit of society.

The word 'company' comes from the Latin *com*, 'with', and *pane*, 'bread': those with whom you share your bread. It implies full human participation, body, mind and spirit and full co-operation with others having a common goal and common responsibilities.

In oriental cultures there is greater acceptance of individuals working as an integral part of a group. As noted, for many companies in Japan, employees were seen as a part of the family. In the West, by contrast, we have become much more concerned with the individual: individual rights, individual performance, and so on. This orientation means that attempting to organize a group of diverse individuals into a coherent business unit that operates as one can be a challenging task.

An example of the different perspectives of the East and the West is that in China the building of the Three Gorges Dam required the uprooting of more than one million people. Some villages with as many as 50,000 inhabitants were told that they had to move to another location; some had to change their means of liveli-hood. In almost all cases the village as a whole, as one, moved. There was minimum disruption because dissent was not permitted. This exemplifies not only the irresistible power of the Chinese state, but also Eastern group loyalty.

Compare that to the scene in England where it took about thirty years to get all the planning permissions in order to build the M25 motorway. Many individuals fought vigorously to defend both their individual rights to remain, and the environment which would be affected by the construction of the motorway. Many people, and in fact the community as a whole, were deprived of the convenience of the road for the sake of individual rights. As British society holds the rights of the individual as important, the long delay was accepted as necessary.

All companies have values that often stem from the principles and values of the founder or in larger entities from the values of the cur-rent management team. Where values have been well established over some time, for example at Cadbury, the current management team acts in ways that they believe are consistent with the founders' values.

It has become fashionable over the last few decades for compa-nies to prepare and publicize a mission statement. For many organ-izations it proved to be a useful exercise to develop such a statement as it required a degree of self-examination. All too often however, the employees were not consulted in the development of the state-ment and the result has been empty words which have had little or no impact on employee behaviour.

This process has also been followed in recent years by the develop-ment of Ethical Codes and CSR statements. Indeed, a growing num-ber of companies are voluntarily reporting information on the 'triple bottom line' i.e. economic, environmental and social performance. The development of such codes is a good first step, but as will be discussed later, it requires a lot of work to put the fine words into practice.

One example of a company statement where significant effort has been expended over a long period to make the words a reality is the 'Credo' of Johnson & Johnson.

Their website describes the role of this statement as follows:

> '. . . for more than 60 years a simple one page document – Our Credo – has guided our actions in fulfilling our responsibilities to our customers, our employees the community and our stockholders. Our worldwide Family of Companies shares this value system in 36 languages spreading across Africa, Asia/Pacific, Eastern Europe, Europe, Latin America, Middle East and North America.'

Here are a few excerpts from the Johnson & Johnson Credo:

> We believe our first responsibility is to the doctors, nurses and patients, to mothers and fathers and all others who use our services.
>
> Our suppliers and distributors must have an opportunity to make a fair profit.
>
> We are responsible to our employees, the men and women who work with us throughout the world.
>
> We must be mindful of ways to help our employees fulfil their family responsibilities.
>
> We must provide competent management, and their actions must be just and ethical.
>
> We are responsible to the communities in which we live and work and to the world community as well.

> Our final responsibility is to our stockholders. Business must
> make a sound profit.
> When we operate according to these principles, the stock-
> holders should realize a fair return.
> (Johnson & Johnson)

Given the longevity of the company, their fine reputation and their continued vitality in the market, one can infer that living the principles outlined in this Credo has had a positive effect on the organization and their employees.

The general picture of big business is not so rosy when one listens to many critics today, who argue that the pendulum has swung closer to the stage where society no longer trusts business to regulate itself. Here are some typical accusations:

- Corporations care little for the welfare of workers, and given the opportunity will move production to sweatshops in less well regulated countries.
- Unchecked, companies will squander scarce natural resources.
- Companies do not pay the full costs of their impact. For example the costs of cleaning up pollution often fall on society in general. As a result profits of corporations are enhanced at the expense of social or ecological welfare.

Among the values which a company supports, there are a few 'core' values that embody the essence of the organization. In their book *Built to Last*, Collins and Porras (1997) compared 18 'visionary companies', which had been operating successfully for at least fifty years, with eighteen of their direct peers, all of which have been well known as relatively successful at certain points of their history. The authors found that a key characteristic in distinguishing the visionary company from its peers was having a core purpose beyond making money. Being clear about this purpose helped visionary companies achieve far greater long-term financial performance than their peers. As a measure of the improved performance it was shown that $1 invested in 1926 in a fund comprised of visionary companies would have grown to $6356 by 1990, compared to $955 for a dollar invested in the comparison group.

Recent research supports their findings. The Institute of Business Ethics published a study of FTSE 250 companies in 2003, showing that those with an ethical code in place for over five years out-performed a similar sized group of companies who said they did not have a code. The survey used as measures economic value added (EVA), market value added (MVA) and price/earnings ratio (P/E). They generated significantly more EVA and MVA than their peers and suffered from much less volatility in their P/E ratios (Institute of Business Ethics, 2003).

For the last seven years studies have been undertaken in the UK exploring spirituality at work, i.e. where the values of the employees have a spiritual aspect. Employees are increasingly searching for more 'meaning' in their work. A *People Management* article in 1998, *Creed is Good*, outlined some of the results. One conclusion was that many younger people were being 'turned off' by the constant pressure to meet targets, the heavy emphasis placed on compensation packages and by the lack of any reference to more deeply-held values to make sense of their hectic working lives. The article suggested that spirituality in work initiatives is being led more by employees than by employers (Welch, 1998).

In a follow-up study in 2003 by the Roffey Park Institute the following results were presented:

- Fifty-three per cent admit to experiencing tension between the spiritual side of their values and their daily work;
- More than forty per cent of UK managers and more than fifty per cent of workers would value the opportunity to discuss workplace spirituality with their customers;
- More than ninety per cent said that their organization had never attempted to make spirituality a topic of discussion at work. (Roffey Park, 2003)

In the USA where a poll was undertaken by Gallup in 2001, the following figures were quoted in a *Fortune* magazine article (Gallup, 2001):

- Seventy-eight per cent of Americans today seek spiritual growth, which is up from twenty percent in 1994;
- Ninety-five per cent of Americans say they believe in God or a universal spirit;
- Forty-eight per cent had talked about faith at work in the past 24 hours;
- Sixty per cent of executives respond favourably to the term 'spirituality'.

While the word 'spirituality' is open to a number of interpretations, in the business context it is generally agreed that employees value 'values'.

As already noted, there are some common principles supported by all the major spiritual traditions; truth, love, justice and freedom, which are the foundation of other human values/virtues such as trust, respect, harmony, tolerance, responsibility and loyalty. A society truly rises to a higher level when these values are put into practice by individuals. It does not achieve such change through mechanical or technological efficiency.

Companies do not bear the primary responsibility for uplifting society, individuals do. It is through their actions and perceptions that organizations can be guided to participate in the process of refinement. A strong moral foundation frees creative energies to enable employees at all levels to work together to make the vision of the company a reality and thus bring value to all.

Principles as the foundation of fine performance

We set out below the basis of an organisation whose foundation is the universal principles and values we have been discussing. While it may be unlikely that you would find such a company, we hope the model will prove a useful framework for the practical examples to follow.

The universal principles

Truth	Justice
Love	Freedom

The eight foundation values

Courage	Respect
Loyalty	Responsibility
Magnanimity	Temperance
Patience	Tolerance

When these principles and values are proclaimed by the leadership, agreed to by all and put into practice in all aspects of the business, then a positive work environment, a culture, is created in the business that is conducive to:

Service	Creative expression
Innovation	Concern for quality
Personal growth	Cooperation

It produces conditions suitable for the development of an effective management team that leads, organizes and teaches effectively. As a group the leaders are:

Visionary	Fair
Virtuous	Personally accountable
Cohesive	Trusted
Open/receptive	Respected
Disciplined	

As a consequence a productive workforce manifests that is:

Honest	Generous
Focussed on service	Efficient
Creative	Responsive
Confident	Enthusiastic
Courageous	Happy

The consequence is that the company delivers value:

Satisfied, loyal staff and customers

Well rewarded investors/shareholders

Valued and reliable suppliers

A reputation as a good place to work

A trusted brand name

Admiration and respect of the community

During the Philosophy in Business courses which we gave at the School of Economic Science in London, we reflected on and discussed the characteristics of a good company. In addition to the six listed above, we also agreed that the following characteristics applied:

Freedom and ability to innovate

Clear vision for the future success of the company

Well considered strategic and tactical plans

Individual contributions valued and acknowledged

Excellent company spirit and unity of purpose

Contribution to and caring for the community

Empowerment of staff at all levels and promotion of individual development

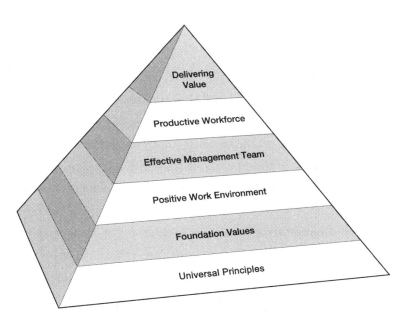

The Value Pyramid

Moral dilemmas

We have presented an ideal conceptual framework of moral principles and how their application can lead to finer company performance. But while we may recognize these principles as true and good, our willingness and resolve to put them into practice consistently will be continually tested. This is a necessary part of the refinement process.

> The gem cannot be polished without friction, nor man perfected without trials.
>
> Chinese proverb, cit. in Mencken, 1946 edn.

Some of the difficulties in deciding on the right course of action come when we need to decide between two principles, both of them good. For example, between:

- Individual and family;
- Company and society;
- Short and long term;
- Justice and mercy;
- Truth and loyalty.

These choices require careful discrimination. The best way to accomplish this is to allow the mind to fall still so that the full implications of the choice can be considered. All too often we undertake such decisions while the mind is in an active and agitated state. A quiet mind creates mental space. Greater clarity is then possible.

Having resolved the dilemma you need the courage to act on the decision. Often the resistance arises in the form of conflicting ideas within oneself. When a decision based on moral principles is put into practice with confidence, the opposing ideas lose some of their power. By the continual application of principles, over time this resistance can be gradually eliminated.

We are warned by various teachers, including Sun Tzu in his treatise *The Art of War* (cit. in Kheng Hor, 1997), about attitudes and behaviours that can prevent the natural qualities from arising. Among the most dangerous are:

- Arrogance: becoming overbearing and presumptuous, usually arising when one has claimed credit for any success. It also shows in someone who is highly sensitive about his or her reputation. This is closely aligned to pride, which is especially damaging in that it closes one to criticism or guidance from others. To avoid being trapped by pride or arrogance, be more fearful of praise than criticism.

- Recklessness: this produces blindness to what is really happening. It usually manifests with a quick temper and debilitating anger. What is lacking is patience and steadfastness. These qualities enable the channelling of the energy in a more productive direction.

- Cowardice: a lack of courage or willingness to do what one knows is right and is needed at the time. At the heart of cowardice is fear. When you examine fear more closely you will find that it always relates to the future and to imagining what might happen. Often cowardice is hidden behind the mask of inactivity. Managers do not make any positive decisions or commitments in case the project should fail.

- Excessive emotion: emotion improperly applied turns to sentimentality, which is a poor reflection of true emotions such as love, compassion and benevolence. Decisions based solely on not wanting to hurt the feelings of another are not usually beneficial to the other person in the long term. Such decisions are actually careless. What is required is a calmness and steadiness which will allow the true emotions to operate naturally.

In order to identify your most difficult obstacles to virtue, you will need to observe yourself in action. Watch the movements in the mind and the emotions as you respond to day-to-day activities. Remind yourself of the moral principles that are your heritage and act from them.

For this approach to be practical, we need to answer the fundamental question posed in the introduction, how one can work to principle while still achieving profitability.

A road map – from principles to profits

It begins with an organization that has:

1. AGREED FOUNDATION PRINCIPLES AND VALUES

These foundation principles and values need to be agreed, communicated and lived.

For such values to become part of the living fabric of the company, the senior executives must set a consistent example through decisions based on principle, and their actions.

Vigilance is required at all levels with special care over decisions that may be made for the sake of short-term success at the expense of the agreed principles.

Agreement on these principles manifests as:

2. CONSISTENT INTERNAL POLICIES AND STANDARDS

The resultant policies and standards will be recognized by all to be fair and responsive to the needs of both the company and the employees. From this a mutual respect develops which grows into a high degree of trust between management and employees.

This foundation of trust is sustained by open and effective internal communications.

This results in:

3. A HIGH LEVEL OF EMPLOYEE AND MANAGEMENT SATISFACTION

People who are secure and happy in their work will be loyal and are less likely to search elsewhere for employment.

With high morale the atmosphere at work becomes positive.

More energy is therefore available for the business.

This enables:

4. HIGH PRODUCTIVITY AND ENTHUSIASM

More and finer energy leads to a better perception of customer needs and of the ways to present the company's capabilities as well as the production of the products and services that meet those needs.

A strong team spirit can then more easily develop, which generates natural enthusiasm.

What also then follows is a disciplined work pattern that avoids wasted energy.

This gives:

5. HIGH QUALITY SERVICE

The aspects of quality that become part of what is expected of everyone in the company are:

- Reliability: we do what we say, consistently
- Assurance: we are there to solve any problems
- Responsiveness: to the inevitable changing needs
- Effectiveness: we deliver results

This produces quite naturally:

6. A HIGH LEVEL OF CUSTOMER SATISFACTION

Like contented employees, satisfied customers will remain so for a long time, which often leads to follow-on business.

Their loyalty acts as a shield against competitive approaches and they stay as customers when times are hard.

Such long-term customers are more willing to provide testimonials and referrals.

This leads to:

7. PROFITS AND GROWTH

The most profitable sales are generally to existing customers, due to lower marketing costs and more intimate knowledge of their needs.

Opportunities open up to serve other parts of the customer organization.

If both parties report a satisfactory relationship, this helps enhance the company's reputation and brand name.

In times of crisis and opportunity, an organization that is founded on these principles and which has established these practices will be more likely to succeed, thanks to its contented and productive workforce, its considerate and trustworthy leadership and its positive attitude towards service.

Let us now look at how the universal moral principles, truth, love, justice and freedom and the eight foundational values can manifest themselves in business.

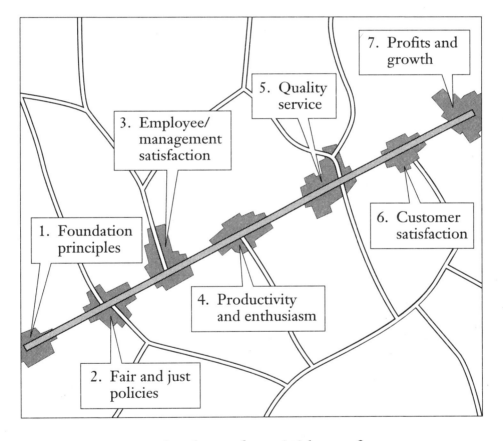

A road map – from principles to profits

CHAPTER 6 - UNIVERSAL PRINCIPLES

Truth is a difficult subject to discuss nowadays. The idea that there is one truth about any subject is not readily accepted. The common idea is that everything is relative: 'What is true for me is my truth and it may well be different from your idea about truth. My view is as good as yours.'

To tell the truth is also not viewed by many as absolute. For many the prohibition of the Ninth Commandment does not seem to carry the same weight as the relativist arguments of today. While it would be generally viewed as acceptable to lie to save someone's life, some people use this extreme exception as the basis for believing that telling the truth is *not* a moral imperative.

The position we hold is that to tell the truth in business is not only necessary, it is essential and natural. We are thus claiming that to tell a lie is unnatural.

What does it feel like when you tell a lie? Do you feel comfortable? Or is there an uneasy heat that builds up inside, an internal agitation? The existence and practical use of lie detectors, mechanical devices which measure the abnormal internal reaction when someone is lying, are another indication of its unnaturalness.

Have you also noted the burden that accumulates when you have to support a lie, usually with more lies and how you must spend a great effort to remember your lies so that you can maintain some semblance of consistency?

There is evidence that the tide is turning, for instance in the public revulsion at the email in which the Exploration Director of

AT WORK: TRUTH

Shell, Walter Van de Vijver wrote to the Chairman, Sir Philip Watts: 'I am becoming sick and tired of lying about the extent of our reserves issues and the downward revisions that need to be done because of far too aggressive/optimistic bookings' (Denning, 2004).

On the other hand to tell the truth is simple and fulfilling. There is of course the art of telling the truth pleasantly in difficult situations so as to minimize the discomfort of others. But if one is committed to the truth then the best way to express it will follow.

The concomitants of truth that most affect us in business are honour, trust and integrity.

Honour

In the city of Baghdad lived Haakem, the wise one. People went to him for counsel which he gave freely to all, asking nothing in return.

There came to him a young man who had spent much but got little and said to Haakem, 'Tell me, wise one, what shall I do to recover the most for that which I spend?'

Haakem answered, 'A thing that is bought or sold has no value unless it contains that which cannot be bought or sold. Look for the Priceless Ingredient.'

'But what is the Priceless Ingredient?' asked the young man.

Spoke then the wise one, 'My son, the Priceless Ingredient of every product in the market place is the

Honour and Integrity of those who sell it. Consider their
name before you buy.'

'The Priceless Ingredient', E R Squibb & Sons, c. 1920

It is obvious, whether your business is a global corporation like
Tesco or you are a greengrocer in a village, that your reputation is
crucial to success. While there are many factors involved in establishing a fine name, a key factor is whether or not you are trusted
by your customers, by your employees and by your suppliers. A reputation can be very fragile as it is being developed and it can easily
be tarnished by the actions of a few.

Companies use mission statements and, more recently, codes of
ethics to try to enhance their reputation in the market. A new book,
The 18 Immutable Laws of Corporate Reputation by Ron Alsop (2005),
highlights examples of ethics codes that give new meaning to the
phrase 'empty words'. The prime example is Enron's ethics code
that read as follows:

We want to be proud of Enron and to know that it enjoys a
reputation for fairness and honesty and that is respected . . .
Let's keep that reputation high . . . Ruthlessness, callousness
and arrogance don't belong here (see Byrne, 2004).

In the not too distant past the basis for most transactions in the
City of London was the statement of honour, 'My word is my
bond'. Very simple, very powerful and for many years the words
meant what they said.

Is it possible to re-kindle this simple basis for business commitments? Here are some ways in which this fine principle of honour-
ing one's word can be used with greater confidence:

● Get to know the people you are dealing with.

- Provide a 100 per cent Guarantee.
- Be willing to pay for the consequences of your failures.
- Take a long term view.
- Be patient.
- Be transparent.
- Be honest about your intentions and expectations.

A friend told us of his commitment to honesty, whatever the cost:

'Six years ago I was Finance Director in an engineering company that was a sub-contractor on Ministry of Defence (MOD) projects. Our new Managing Director had delivered quotations to the prime contractor on a major MOD contract worth around £15 million. The nature of the work quoted gave my company the status of sole supplier, but with this status came the responsibility of quoting a price within the constraints of the MOD rules for single source supply.

'The Managing Director had no intention of quoting a price that was within the MOD's strict pricing rules. I had hoped that during the negotiations the prime contractor would identify that the prices quoted were far too high but unfortunately he did not. Several times I had tried to persuade the Managing Director that it was ethically incorrect and not in the company's best interests to behave in this way, but he was not prepared to change his approach.

As Finance Director, and responsible for all commercial contracts, it fell to me to sign off on the official contract that the company was fully compliant with all the MOD rules. I refused to sign the documents and effectively resigned from the company. I was nearing my fiftieth birthday and in a well paid, secure job which I had enjoyed. As I look back, I am one hundred per cent confident that I took the correct action and I have never regretted it.'

Trust

Honesty binds. The binding is called trust. It is crucial to every kind of business. No trust, no business.

In lectures on *Trust in Business* and *Trust Between Citizens* at the Royal Society of Arts in 2005 David Halpern of the Prime Minister's Strategy Unit (Halpern, 2005) and Philip Dewhurst, Group Director Corporate Affairs, for BNFL (Dewhurst, 2005), presented conclusions on trust drawn from the results of a MORI poll and other sources on the importance of honesty in the establishment and maintenance of a company's reputation in the community.

Some of the results were striking: over the last 20 years there has been a distinct shift in the importance of honesty as a prime criterion for evaluating a company's reputation.

In 1969 . . . honesty was a given. These days . . . it is no longer taken for granted. 52% bought from a company because of good reputation, 44% did not buy from a company because of its reputation. People are voting with their feet!

Institute of Business Ethics, 2003

Ninety-two per cent of the respondents to the MORI survey said they trusted doctors (despite the breach of trust by the mass murderer, Dr Harold Shipman) and sixty-nine per cent trusted scientists, but only thirty per cent trusted business leaders, just ahead of the twenty-two per cent who trusted politicians. Only eleven per cent thought that directors could be trusted to tell the truth, while eighty percent thought that they could not (Dewhurst, 2005).

The issue of honesty or integrity is an increasingly important factor in people's judgement of a company's reputation. In 1984, only ten per cent rated honesty or integrity as one of the most important things to know about a company in making that judgement, much less than the quality of its products or services (thirty-five per cent) and customer service (eighteen per cent). It was largely taken for granted. By 2004, quality of service as a criterion had dropped to twenty-one per cent while honesty or integrity had risen to twenty-five per cent: clear evidence of increasing concern about the integrity of businesses and the deterioration in their reputation generally. Directors of companies are seriously mistrusted by the public (Halpern, 2005).

Among analysts, who have significant influence on the share prices of the companies they follow, the survey showed that forty-seven per cent felt that openness, honesty and telling the truth created trust among analysts. Thirty-six per cent rated delivering on promises while only ten per cent said that financial performance engenders trust (Halpern, 2005).

These studies provide a clear picture as to the conditions in the UK. Given our global perspective of business, what is the attitude in other countries regarding general human trust? The survey data showed that around sixty-five per cent of people in Scandinavian countries said that 'most people can be trusted'. In Asian countries such as China, Indonesia, Japan, Vietnam and India forty to fifty-five per cent of people held the same view. In Anglo-Saxon countries including Australia, Canada, the USA, Ireland and Britain, as well as Germany, Italy Spain and Belgium, the figure was thirty to forty per cent In the former Soviet Union it was down to between fifteen and thirty per cent in Central and South America less than twenty-five per cent and in Southern Africa less than fifteen per cent (Dewhurst, 2005).

There is a problem: business and business leaders have lost the trust of the public that they serve. As Dr. Onora O'Neill pointed out in her 2002 BBC Reith Lectures, business is not the only institution to have lost trust. In politics and public service, the professions and journalism, the loss of trust has been widespread. It is very difficult for the other institutions to operate without trust or with reduced trust. It is impossible for business (O'Neill, 2002).

Building trust

How does one re-establish trust, both within and without the organization? Establishing trust in a company requires not only effective leadership, but also a strong statement of principles, integrated training and clear communications.

In our Philosophy in Business courses we discussed at some length the ways to establish and maintain trust. The list that follows arose from the more than 100 managers who attended the courses:

How to build trust	Some practical measures
Be courageous	Let go of fear, take some risk. Do not hesitate to do what you know is right. Stand up against wrong.
Be honest and clear	Don't skirt round the difficult issues. Be straight about expectations.

Be open	Don't hide problems; share information and knowledge.
Be selfless	Take care of everyone else. Be willing to sacrifice your own interests.
Communicate effectively	Speak when it is appropriate, listen carefully and fully, and learn all the time.
Go the extra mile	Try to exceed the expectations of others. Provide more than you have to.
Acknowledge efforts	Give praise and thanks where they are due.
Be fair	Seek the solution that is equitable for all.
Be consistent	Adhere constantly to true principles of thought, speech and action.
Discriminate	Discern the truth in a situation and act on it. To do this you have to be in the present and ignore pre-conceptions.

In the end being trustworthy comes down to being fully consistent: As you think, speak, and as you speak, act.

A friend of ours paints a beautiful picture of the sanctity of trust in the jewellery business:

> 'I have now worked in the jewellery trade for seventeen years and I knew from the first day that its success was solely due to complete trust in your colleagues, suppliers and customers. We all still hand over to each other gems and jew-

ellery sometimes worth hundreds of thousands of pounds, with a hand shake. If that were to be stolen by the recipient, the giver would never be able to prove the transaction. Reputation is everything; we assume someone is honest. If we do not know them, a phone call to a mutual contact is all that is needed to reassure one of the person's integrity. It is the most wonderful way to conduct business and consequently it is a close and happy community. Once a reputation is lost then their business is lost with it. If we had to write every transaction down as a lawful contract we would be finished. Our contract and obligation are understood without words.

'A teacher once said to me that the first principle in any career or job was service and then profits would follow. That is so useful to remember, especially when times are hard but it has proved its worth. All the fly-by-nights come and go but to keep going despite the pressures of losing our manufacturing base to the Middle and Far East, and retailers suffering in the High Street is actually due to that principle, as it produces loyalty and mutual support.

'There have been several occasions over the years when a supplier has lost or broken a piece entrusted to my care. My assistant recently mislaid two tie clips which I have had to replace and it has cost me £1000. It would not cross my mind to renege on our verbal agreement, but without asking for it I know my customer will subsequently support me in the future.

'When I took on my assistant, business was busy and I

offered him 12 months employment. Shortly thereafter my largest customer, who provided seventy per cent of my turnover, was bought out and I lost the contract. Consequently not only did I not have much work for him but it was very difficult to pay him! Nevertheless it was right not to let him go early as I had given my word, and he has seen that to live and work by your word is crucial to everyone's well-being.

'Finally I love my work because it allows me to provide something that is loved by the recipient and many good friendships have arisen from this. Customers are not stupid and know that they will be better served when their interests are at the supplier's heart and they can tell when that happens. In addition jewellery at its best is that wonderful combination of the best that nature can offer up and the best creative skills of the artisan. It is a manifestation of harmony.'

You can see the importance of knowledge about principles. When a principle is fully accepted in the mind as true, you are then naturally able to speak from this knowledge. When you speak the truth, the power is there to put the words into action. This is how principles are put into practice.

To live in this way requires a firm resolve, a conscious decision to be truthful. In his *Seven Spiritual Steps to Success*, Deepak Chopra lists such a conscious choice as one of the key steps. In every moment there is choice. We can either go with a habitual, mechanical response or we can wake up to the possibilities of the moment. Chopra says:

There is only one choice that will create happiness for you

and for those around you. When you make that choice it will result in a form of behaviour that is called spontaneous right action – right action at the right moment.

Chopra, *Seven Spiritual Steps to Success*, 1994

We each need to make a decision to act morally and then manage our lives based on that decision. We cannot manage the consequences of decisions we haven't made.

An article in *The Times* in September 2000 referred to a web search using the words 'unethical business' that threw up 63,797 responses (Cullingford, 2000). In September 2005 the same search produced 1,130,000 responses. Search engines have become more efficient in this period and the web has grown, but the trend is nevertheless worrying.

A cursory review of the most prominent references reveals a growing concern and frustration with the actions of business people in a wide range of industries and countries. More people seem now to be engaging in petty but pervasive actions such as fiddling expenses, copying, that is to say stealing, software and using the company's resources such as office supplies unlawfully. Most disturbing is the proliferation of the more high profile and serious violations of trust by senior executives and board members. This latter category is doubly damaging in that it sets the worst possible example for the employees as well as damaging the reputations of the companies involved.

At the World Economic Forum at Davos in 2005 sixty-three major corporations signed up to a zero tolerance pact to counter bribery. This particular form of corruption drains the life from markets, preventing their efficient operation and sowing an atmosphere of mistrust. This agreement is important but business must fulfil such commitments. If trust is to be forged anew, business leaders must act on their good intentions. Such an agreement can give great strength to those who signed, in that they are now working as a group to counter this negative force. But if there is no follow-up then the consequences will be very damaging and an opportunity will be lost. The world is watching (Duncan, 2005).

The 'dot.com' bubble that burst at the turn of the century caused a great loss of wealth for investors, but more importantly a loss of faith and confidence in the investment and corporate communities. The numerous instances of greed and deception left many private investors in a quandary as to where they might invest to earn sufficient for their retirement. There have recently been calls from academics, economists and market practitioners for those in the financial markets to consider afresh their ethical responsibilities. It is not sufficient to act lawfully; they must act morally.

In an increasingly familiar argument, the case is being made that a market known to be secure and to be run along ethical principles will be more trusted by investors. It will therefore be larger and more inclusive than otherwise, attracting a wider range of participants. And since bigger, deeper markets are more efficient and more liquid, they will offer a more diverse and cheaper range of financial options for those who use them. Everyone wins.

One scandal of major concern to the financial markets was that involving Citigroup. When the world's biggest bank, consisting of 20 financial services companies, employing 294,000 people and with an annual turnover of $108 billion is hit by scandal, everyone takes notice. The bank is taking drastic steps to restore its tarnished reputation. A programme devised and backed by the management committee of the bank includes an expanded training programme in corporate ethics, better internal communications, greater focus on talent and development, a new performance appraisal and compensation system and tighter internal controls. Thus the bank recognized that the steps to tighten up on ethical issues needed to be supported by a strategy to enhance internal staff development and that action was needed across the group (Butcher, 2005).

There is a major international problem with bribery, affecting not only the USA, and countries such as Nigeria and Russia, but also a country like Germany, previously regarded as relatively free from corruption. There have been bribery scandals recently at Volkswagen, Daimler–Chrysler and BMW that have exposed significant corruption in that country. One economist estimated that $50 million in bribes are paid every year in Germany (Boyes, 2005). Other casualties of the major corporate scandals have been the large accountancy firms whose credibility has been called into question. The collapse of Arthur Andersen in 2002, then one of the 'big five' accounting firms, was a conspicuous example. Anything that threatens a loss of trust in the professions is a real cause for concern as the whole relationship between the client and a member of the professions depends upon it.

Integrity

The word 'integrity' is derived from the Latin *'integritas'* which means wholeness or completeness. It has also come to mean honesty. From it we have the word 'integral' – making up a whole, parts that together constitute a unity. An individual's integrity is characterized by thoughts, words and actions that are truthful and consistent. In practice this means that such a person is honest, transparent, responsible, caring and worthy of respect. It is someone who does what he says.

In a report, *Corporate Integrity: The Strategic Reality* the meaning and basis of corporate integrity was presented in the form of Six Pillars (Minton & Blagg, 2004):

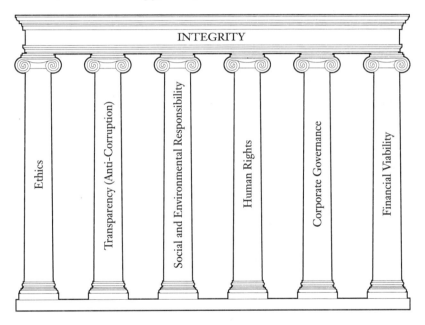

The Six Pillars of Corporate Integrity

- Ethics
- Transparency (Anti-Corruption)
- Social and Environmental Responsibility
- Human Rights
- Corporate Governance
- Financial Viability

In the foreword to that report Paul Walsh, CEO of Diageo, wrote,

> We understand that acting with integrity is an essential factor in our sustainability and that, without it, our business will not prosper in the long term. Integrity is a cornerstone of the way we do business - we see it simply as good business sense.
>
> Cit. in Minton & Blagg, 2004

To integrate these pillars into the fabric of a company requires that they be fully aligned with the company's publicly declared strategy, values and management practices.

A criticism levelled against well-meaning CSR programmes is that they are either incomplete in their scope or that they are impractical. Michael Porter, the internationally known management guru, focuses his comments on the latter:

> My major criticism is that the field of corporate social responsibility has become a religion, in which there is no need for evidence or theory. Too many academics and business managers are satisfied with the 'good feeling' of the argument.
>
> Cit. in Littlechild, 2003/4

The head of CSR policy at the European Commission has stated that the time for discussing the business case for CSR is over: the business case argument for doing the right thing is a good start but it is not enough. Individuals and organizations should do what is right because it is the right thing to do, not because it pays (Simms, 2002).

This lack of follow-through by companies, not putting the well-meaning words into action constitutes a lack of integrity. Completeness is missing. It requires work.

Paul writes:

> My company, founded in 1987, had survived in the highly competitive, technology-driven industry of computer-based training (now called e-learning). In the early years of the business there were only between three and five people involved, including my wife, but as the company grew external investors were brought in, recruitment became an important activity and we felt the need to be more formal in our statement of vision, values and policies.
>
> After much discussion, we, all the employees, concluded that 'integrity' and 'service' were the basis upon which we had been working and we agreed on them as our core values. We recognized that they would have to be fully accepted by people we hired and by those who represented us in other territories (our resellers). These values also represented a promise to all those who dealt with us, i.e. our investors, suppliers, clients, and so on. While it may appear to some that by committing to such values, you are sticking your neck out, to us it seemed to be a statement of what we believed was natural.
>
> It became our practice to ask people being interviewed for employment what they understood by integrity and what good service meant to them. We found it to be a good way to discuss with them what we expected of employees and to get some indication of their individual values.
>
> On more than one occasion an employee asked for some

guidance on the practical application of integrity. Over the years the word took on new meaning as we were faced with a wide variety of new situations where it was necessary to resort to our values for guidance.

It came to mean, among other things, keeping your word. If we committed to a delivery date, we had to meet that date even if other business opportunities appeared that would mean diverting resources. As a small company we had to optimise the use of our valuable resources, so there were times when we had to ask the company to whom we committed a date, whether it would be possible to slip it for a specific period. If they agreed we made the change, if not we kept to our original commitment.

A commitment came to be seen as a promise by the company and no one likes to break a promise. This principle made us wary of being too quick with our commitments, even in the white heat of competitive negotiations.

In one case we were dealing with a reseller operating in a country where bribery was common. We were faced with the proposition that unless our reseller paid the bribe our courses would not operate on a system installed in a number of prime accounts. We gave instructions to the reseller not to pay the bribe and managed to contact a very senior manager in the organization that employed the person demanding the bribe. We were able to generate enough pressure to get the threat removed. Unless our resolve not to pay had been strong, the creative solution to the problem would not have appeared.

I would not say that we had a perfect record of keeping precisely to all our commitments, but a way of working emerged that would not allow us to act irresponsibly for the sake of the short term gain.

An American business colleague writes of putting the needs of the customer before her own:

'I am an author and advisor on economic value management and corporate governance. I was approached about five years ago by an investment banker from one of the leading banks and an analyst at a major credit risk rating agency. They were interested in going into business with me, offering securitization products to banks and other financial institutions. [Note: Securitization is a financial technique that pools together assets such as a mortgage book, and, in effect, turns them into a security which can be traded.] They wanted my assistance because they knew I was well known as a proponent of value concepts and would be a great spokesperson for the economic value of the transactions that would be proposed.

'However I had spent some time studying the economics of securitization through previous work I had done and I knew that on the whole the benefits on a risk-adjusted or economic basis did not accrue to the buyers of the instruments, but rather to the sellers. In essence I was being asked to use my name to promote a product that I knew would not be in the best interest of the customer.

'So I said to them, "Are you asking me to promote this product even though it is most often not in the best interest of the customer?" "Yes," they said. Then the customers were not being truly served. Of course, I had no further discussions with them about the idea and I did not do it, although I surely could have made a lot of money if I had. Without my support for the idea, they did not pursue it either.'

We shall now consider the second of the foundation virtues, love. You don't hear much about love in business but it is fundamental to the operation of any company and it informs all the relationships within the company and with everyone that deals with it.

CHAPTER 7 - UNIVERSAL PRINCIPLES

As we showed in the descriptions of the various moral teachings, love in all its forms is the foundation of virtue. The importance is highlighted in the Judaeo-Christian teaching as 'Love thy neighbour as thy self', in the compassion of the Buddha and in the importance of *ren* in the Confucian tradition. There is no mistaking this direction.

All business activities involve relationships. Our attitude towards 'the other' will be reflected in all that we think, say and do. We need to consider both our relationships within the organization and with those outside it. If we are not careful we could fall into the trap of behaving in one way to the external world and using another set of standards internally. This 'double standard' may also be manifest when we act in one way with our family and friends and in another with those with whom we work. Before long there will be so many different standards of behaviour that an inevitable tension and confusion will arise. This uncertainty and doubt will eventually mar our relationships, making trust difficult if not impossible to maintain.

Another dimension of the case for compassion has been voiced by Sander Tideman in his book, *Mind over Matter*:

> We can understand the need for values such as compassion because of mutual dependence in this increasingly smaller and interconnected world. But spiritual traditions point to another, more profound and personal dimension of compassion. They advise us to make altruism the core of our practice, not only because it is the cheapest and most effective

AT WORK: LOVE

insurance policy for our future, but also specifically because the real benefit of compassion is that it will bring about a transformation in the mind of the practitioner. It will make us happy.

Sander Tideman, *Mind Over Matter*, 2005

In terms of business relationships, one of the most pressing issues is the relationship between management and employees. At one extreme are those situations where employees are exploited. This does not only refer to sweatshops in developing countries but also to those organizations where financial performance is the ruling dictate. In a ruthless search for efficiency, relationships are often pushed aside or ignored. Another level according to Charles Handy, a well known business consultant, is when companies treat their employees as mercenaries. They are employed for a particular task and then turned out when the task is completed. The current trend towards outsourcing is encouraging this type of attitude as the company becomes once-removed from a direct relationship with the employees.

A third view, one supported by Handy, is that the employees are citizens of a company, people who feel proud to march under the company's banner, who speak of 'our company' and see management as part of 'us' rather than 'them'. (Handy, 1997). What is often overlooked in the rush for efficiency and short-term gain is the energy and power that manifests when a person is committed and loyal. When employees identify their future with that of the company, when the relationship is close, the quality of the work is bound to be finer.

We need to examine relationships in a wider context. We have set out a premise that the role of business in society is to create wealth for the sake of all. Do you believe that you are actually working for the benefit of all – that you as an individual, your family and fellow employees are part of that all?

What is the degree of your compassion towards those who are not as well provided as you are? Do you believe that you have any responsibility to others? 'Am I my brother's keeper?' is an age-old question which needs to be answered by each individual in every age.

Compassion

> Compassion is by nature peaceful and gentle, but is also very powerful. It is the true sign of inner strength.
>
> The Dalai Lama, cit. in Bunson, 1997

We should ask ourselves the question, 'For whose benefit is the enterprise in which I am engaged?' If I am an employee, the question is, 'For whom am I working?' If you have management responsibility in an organization you could pose the question, 'To whom are our products or service dedicated?'

Let us look first at the motivations of our actions in life in general and then we will apply the same analysis to the workplace.

It begins with a small circle with 'Me' in the middle. This represents the situation where you act solely for your own benefit – you serve Me. 'I am the main beneficiary; my advancement, my enhancement, my pleasure are what matter.' It is a rather small and limited perspective.

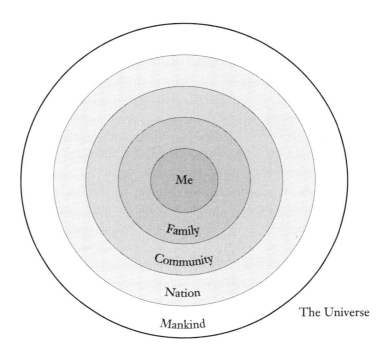

Who is being served?

Some might say – 'Isn't that true all the time for everyone?' We suggest that while this picture does describe our intentions a great deal of the time, there are occasions when the view widens.

The next stage is another circle which represents 'family'. When the limits around 'me' are removed, you become part of a larger circle, in the first case a family. This represents that state when your thoughts, speech and actions are devoted to the service of the family - your wife, husband, children, parents, grandparents, etc. We have all experienced this expansion. What happens is that the boundary that limited attention to 'me' dissolves and you take in something larger quite naturally. When you are in this state, what does it feel like? Isn't it a most natural response to a need to 'sacrifice' your own concerns for that of your child? It is important to note that 'me' is still part of the whole, called 'family' – number one is still being looked after.

> What is a family? It is a place where we feel an atmosphere
> of love and unity.
>
> Swami Prajanpad, in *Indian Wisdom*, 2003

The next stage is 'community'. It can be the community where you live, the company you work for, the club in which you are a member or the charity that you serve. Here again we see the same principle – there is an apparent sacrifice of my own time, energy, or even money. There may be less time with the family for the sake of what is seen as a greater good. This stage is only valid if your true motivation is for the good of the community. Some people participate actively at this level but all the time the inner intention and motivation is still Me. They are really still operating within the small circle of 'Me'. Do not ignore the positive impact of working for a higher goal.

> Seventy-four per cent of companies surveyed agree that
> employees doing volunteer work in the community increases
> employee productivity.
>
> Points of Light Foundation, Study, 1999

Going further, you can act for the sake of the nation. Times of disaster, crisis and war on one hand or competing for your country in sporting events on the other, offer many examples of people realising higher human potential inspired by this wider view. Competing for your country at the Olympics certainly adds another dimension to the games. The players dig deeper into their inner resources and are more motivated because the honour and reputation of the nation as well as their own and the team's is at stake. This can also apply in business and even in politics:

> It was amid these facts and looming prospects that I entered
> upon my duties as Prime Minister and Minister of Defence,
> and addressed myself to the first task of forming a govern-
> ment of all parties to conduct His Majesty's business at home
> and abroad by whatever means might be deemed best suited
> to the National interest.
>
> Winston Churchill, *Their Finest Hour*, 2002 edn.

Other examples of work at this level are those great teachers and leaders in all civilizations who have worked tirelessly for the benefit of mankind. It is their living examples that have given their teachings authority and given confidence for those that followed.

> Duties to self, to the family, to the country and the world are
> not independent of one another. One cannot do good to the
> country by injuring himself or his family. Similarly one can-
> not serve the country by injuring the world at large.
>
> Mahatma Gandhi, in *Indian Wisdom*, 2003

Albert Einstein summed up the message of love and compassion in a way that is as applicable to business as to any other sphere:

> A human being is part of the whole, called by us 'universe',
> a part limited in time and space. He experiences himself, his
> thoughts and feelings as something separated from the rest
> – a kind of optical delusion of his consciousness. This delu-
> sion is a kind of prison for us, restricting us to our personal
> desires and to affection for a few persons nearest to us. Our

task must be to free ourselves from this prison by widening
our circle of compassion to embrace all living creatures and
the whole of nature in its beauty.

As can be seen from the diagram, if we are able to widen our circle of compassion, we shall not only benefit those on the outer reaches but also all those within the smaller circles, including 'Me'.

This approach works equally well in the context of a business operating in a community. At the centre of this new diagram is also 'Me'.

When you, as an employee, are totally motivated by self-interest, what is best for you, then you are living in a very small circle, a small world. All your actions are aimed at securing the best returns for you, your pay packet, your advancement and so on. While this may appear to be the formula for success, experience has shown that the person who is totally focused on self-advancement usually lacks the support of others that is necessary for success in the long term.

The circle can open up to the next level (equivalent to 'family') which represents the smallest business unit. It might be your department, a regional office or a business unit of a larger group. Now you are motivated to achieve the unit goals and your thoughts and energies are turned to ways in which the unit can succeed. There will often be internal competition with other units as you vie for resources, plaudits and rewards.

In making this shift, personal goals are no longer the only motivation. They are not fully ignored but if you have truly moved to this new level, you will be willing to sacrifice your own small interests for the sake of the unit. You might, for example, spend time training a new person in the unit, using time that could have been

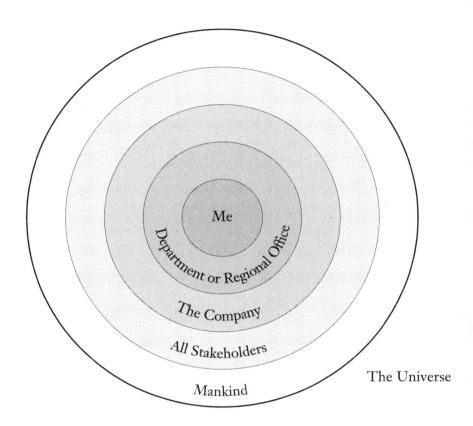

Creating wealth for the benefit of all

expended on your own activities. The shift in priorities is especially noted when the push is on for the unit to meet its performance targets.

If you are able to expand beyond the circle of the unit, the next level is the company as a whole, made up of a number of business units (like 'community'). At this level you need to be concerned about the needs of the company and its overall performance. The better you perform as a unit the better it is for the company, but there are also times when you may be asked to sacrifice the short-term gains of the unit for the benefit of the company. For example, you may need to apply the resources of your unit to assist another part of the company without any recompense. While you may be ordered to do this, the real test is your personal attitude that lies behind the compliance. If you have truly moved to the higher level then your response will be whole-hearted. In fact the suggestion may come from you. Gone are competitive posturing and calcula-tions about the impact of decisions on your unit. It needs to be remembered that if the company as a whole flourishes, then the units and all the individuals also benefit.

It is the mark of a great team or an excellent company when team or company 'spirit' is strong and consistent. This spirit, which with effort can be maintained over a long period, sustains an enter-prise and enhances its reputation. It also makes the company very attractive and many desire to be associated with it.

The next stage (akin to 'nation') is to recognize that the com-pany operates in a large community and has many responsibilities. This includes a group of stakeholders who are dependent to one degree or another on the activities of the company: suppliers, cus-tomers, investors and society at large. This is a major step and when your vision expands to include the needs of this group, the quality of your response to daily activities takes on an entirely different hue.

The duties of the company include care for the environment, labour practices, ethics and social responsibility. The numerous CSR programmes testify to the general recognition of this dimen-sion. You are suddenly looking at a much larger picture and while you may not be personally responsible for any of these areas, you may well be able to make a contribution to help the company fulfil its obligations. Individuals who operate in this mode find that their perspective of business life widens, much like the expanded view of the countryside one gets by climbing a mountain and looking down on it.

You will find yourself asking such questions as, 'How will my decision affect: the environment, or our investors or the community that depends on us for employment?'. The short-term day-to-day activities will still be in focus but there will also be a concern for the wider and longer-term implications.

The final stage in 'widening our circles of compassion' is when you consider the full responsibility of the company, as part of the business community, whose role is to create wealth for the benefit of all. At this stage you go beyond the concerns of the immediate company stakeholders and consider the needs of 'all'.

The recent, highly-publicized initiatives of developed countries to help fight poverty through loan cancellation and moves by governments and companies to increase the import of goods from developing countries are examples of efforts to widen the view to embrace the needs of mankind. As an individual employee you can make a contribution by becoming the eyes and ears of the company to ascertain what contribution might be made to serve those in real need in the locations where you conduct business. A sense of solidarity with all can grow at this stage. When it matures, it will show itself in the nature of the business decisions as well as decisions designed for instance, to help those in need to learn skills that would enable them eventually to be self-sufficient. Corporate philanthropy is another aspect of the response to the needs of others. It is at this point that you and your organization have broken all the circles and are truly fulfilling your role in society.

This approach – to widen the circle – is a very practical matter. This was Chris's experience:

> Some years ago I was managing director of the software products subsidiary of a big IT systems company. Although we had had some success and the business had been profitable for a few years, it had started to lose money because we could not compete with the level of innovation that our much larger American competitors could introduce into their products. I came to the reluctant conclusion that the business had no future and recommended to the board that we stop developing the product, which in software products sounds the death knell for it.
>
> I knew that this decision would have far-reaching effects, on my staff, on the company's morale, possibly its reputation and on our customers, many of which were national defence institutions. With my management team I secretly planned and put in place a programme to take care of everyone. Almost all the staff and the management team were offered roles elsewhere in the company. We put in place a support function to enable the customers to move to other products at their own pace. Then I made the announcement and the plan was implemented. My team were shocked by the decision but felt cared for.
>
> The one person I determined to do nothing for was myself. However, a little while later, I was headhunted and

offered a partnership in a major consulting firm. So I too was cared for by the larger circle, though not in the way I had expected. It is often so.

There have been a number of experiences and lessons learned along the way that have been instrumental in bringing us to write this book. One such was more than forty years ago at Paul's university graduation ceremony. At that event those of us who had completed a four-year degree programme in engineering were asked to pronounce as a group the 'Engineer's Oath', a sort of Hippocratic equivalent for the engineer. The oath formed an impressive part of the final ceremony that helped launch us into the world of work.

Here are some excerpts from the oath that touch on this theme of considering for whose benefit we work. Note: when you hear the word 'engineer' you can substitute 'marketing executive', 'lawyer', 'software developer' or any responsible function.

The Engineer's Oath

As an engineer, I have deep respect and faith in the ideals of my chosen profession; I believe that membership in it entails the most solemn obligations – obligations that I am eager and earnest to fulfil. I believe that, as a member of this profession, I have a vital and personal responsibility to act for the benefit of mankind.

As an engineer, I believe I should dedicate my efforts to the furtherance and development of these ideals and the dissemination of our philosophy and practice to young people of the profession.

As an engineer, I believe, in common with all men, that

I should strive for the common good, interest myself in the service of humanity, and render to my fellow man and to my community without thought of material recompense such service as will be for the greatest public good.

As an engineer, I further believe that my profession requires in its very nature particular sensitivity to moral obligations and to the broadest human welfare and progress, that our world, with its material things and things of the mind and of the spirit, may be a better place to live in.

All these things I do truly believe and to these principles I solemnly commit myself.

Newark College of Engineering, 1960

This oath points to a service that is provided for the benefit of society and to self-regulation as the means for discerning appropriate action. There is an underlying assumption that the individual is a responsible person who will be sensitive to moral obligations and to the welfare of others, even in the face of opposing trends in society or current norms. These obligations, presented in this light, are natural, that is, consistent with man's nature and the oath simply serves as a reminder of that which we know. Given the state of society today where the main concern of the majority seems to be for 'me and mine', we need to be reminded of these principles again and again.

Benevolence

On the subject of benevolence, which is very important in the execution of our responsibilities as managers, it is helpful to look to the East and the teachings of Confucius for some guidance. Of all the qualities and virtues of men Confucius esteemed as greatest what he called *ren*, which is interpreted as benevolence, human-heartedness, goodness. For Confucius this term represented the essence of being a good person. Although it was a noble ideal for him and not easily realized, he taught that it could be found very close at hand, as close as oneself.

> Is goodness far away? If we really wanted goodness, we should find that it is right here.
>
> Confucius, *Analects*, 1971 edn.

Being benevolent was the basis of character and pre-requisite to other subjects of study because of its importance.

> If a man is not good, what has he to do with the rules of propriety (justice)?
>
> Confucius, *Analects*, 1971 edn.

While Confucius did say that 'He whose heart is set upon goodness will dislike no one,' he also said that a good man could not be deceived because of his knowledge of human nature and his attention in the moment. His responses would be appropriate and not sentimental. A good man is also able to discern the qualities in people and act appropriately.

Benevolence, he taught, is a stabilizing yet adaptable quality within man. It enables him to overcome difficulties and sustain success; therefore it is wise to pursue goodness. 'Without goodness a man cannot endure adversity for long, nor can he enjoy prosperity for long.' The good man is naturally at ease with goodness. 'Imperturbable, enduring, simple, slow to speak – such a one is near to goodness.'

Above all, benevolence manifests as correct conduct and behaviour whether in private or public life.

'Behave when away from home as though you were in the presence of an honoured guest. Employ the people as though you were assisting at an important sacrifice. Do not do to others what you would not like yourself. Then there will be no feelings of opposition to you, whether it is the affairs of a state that you are handling or the affairs of a family.'

Confucius, *Analects*, 1971 edn..

Thus goodness can go beyond improving oneself to actually helping others to improve themselves, but it must begin within oneself in order for one to know how to help others. By knowing what is within ourselves we can know others; knowing ourselves, we can improve ourselves and then benefit others also.

'Love' is not a word you hear frequently in the business world, but that does not mean that it is absent. Some of our friends wrote eloquently of the power of love in their business dealings.

'When a sailing ship sank at sea together with its cargo, the commercial loss to the owners and merchants at home could be disastrous. The marine community got together and, in a coffee shop called Lloyds, formulated a principle that "the contributions of the many should pay for the losses of the few". This works only because of the underlying principle "Love thy neighbour as thyself". This is a unity and like all unities has a three-fold aspect: the contributions of the many, the insured, the management of the project, the insurer, and the capitalization of the project by the shareholder. As can be seen, the work of the insurer and the investment of the shareholder are also contributing to the losses of the few.

'This is the basis of the insurance market. It is vital that the underlying principle is not forgotten by all three participants.

'Profit is necessary to enable the project to expand and allow shareholders a proper return on their investment. If excessive profit is sought it will be to the detriment of the losses of the few. Fraudulent claims will deplete the funds for the genuine loss. Equally if the insurer deliberately lowers premiums to bring in business and seeks wherever possible to repudiate claims, it brings the industry into disrepute and the insured suffer the consequences.

'The insurer has a three-part function: the underwriter to assess the risk and calculate the appropriate premium, the business department to bring in new business and maintain existing contacts, and the claims department to meet the needs of the insured.

'Throughout more than forty years in the insurance business mostly spent in investigating and negotiating settlement of, in the main, legal liability claims, the above principle has been my guiding light, especially when due to pressure of work or time it can be tempting to take unreasonable short cuts.

'There is another important principle which applies to the investigator/negotiator. The work entails meeting people from all walks of life, from militant dockers in London to judges in chambers (who also make claims!). It is important to respect the part played by the interviewee, but never to confuse the person with the part. This enables one to see the other as in fact no different from oneself and to expect the truth to be spoken. This is not the naive position it is thought to be, because in this view any untruth stands out. If, on the other hand, you assume the other is a rogue, you are constantly seeking the untruth and the truth can be missed.

'Finally, instead of seeking ways to avoid payment, it is far more efficient to establish quickly whether there is liability under the policy and if so to settle as quickly as possible, or repudiate giving full and clear reasons why. Working in this way gave me considerable job satisfaction.'

Here is another view, also from the insurance industry:

'I am the Chairman of an insurance broking firm, which was originally a family business. Our guiding principle is that the ethical basis for all client service is: "Love thy neighbour as thyself". When this lives in the heart then service arises naturally.

When I came into the family business, my father gave me two pieces of advice:

● First, look after the client and the commission looks after itself.

● Second, although your duty is to your client, try to make sure that the Insurers (the suppliers) make money on your account.

'As an insurance broker, we occupy the middle ground between client and the insurance company. In order to offer a first-class service to clients, not only must there be this natural desire to be of service, there must also be the highest level of professional competence. Without that competence, service is pretty meaningless. In our business, we need to be conversant with policy wordings, fully understand the terms and conditions and limitations, and be able to explain these to our clients in clear layman's terms. We even need to have the ability to draft a policy wording from scratch, to insure a specific one-off type of risk.

'Being a service industry, it is essential for us to employ those who actually like their fellow man! Academic qualifications are valuable but do not of themselves qualify an individual to be a good insurance broker – a good insurance broker is one who puts his client first, not his own wallet, and has the ability to deliver to his client a product which is correctly and professionally structured.

'Being positioned between the client and the supplier brings a broker responsibility in both directions. Trust is absolutely fundamental to our business. Trust is always earned. It arises in a most practical way out of loving thy neighbour as thyself and brings out the best in both parties.

'Respect is also enormously important. We transact much of our business overseas in locations where cultural values differ from ours. Some understanding of these cultural values and a respect for them generates goodwill, friendship, and trust. For example, we have three offices in India and my familiarity with some of India's spiritual and cultural traditions has enabled a strong bond to develop with the individuals with whom we do business. Basic good manners (often forgotten) are also evidence of courtesy and respect.

'Creativity is essential to any business endeavour. Creativity is always spontaneous, arises out of the situation and is never mechanical. People need space to be creative and there is nothing that dulls creativity more than dogma and fixed ideas. In our business, the creative people are those who meet their clients with an open mind, hear what they have to say, and then develop an insurance product which genuinely reflects that client's specific needs.

'How do you become a 'moral manager'? This has nothing to do with putting up some sort of moralistic show. It is all about living according to your values – at home, at work, and at leisure. If these values are good, then you can lead and manage people effectively. If they are selfish, then the lack of morality will permeate the whole life, including the management and leadership of others.'

Let us now look at the impact of putting into practice the other foundation values.

CHAPTER 8 - OTHER UNIVERSAL

Justice

When one hears the word justice, what may come to mind is its application in the courts. Justice in that context is the process by which those who are accused of violating the law are tried and judged, or by which disputes are resolved in the civil courts. These are important aspects of justice but the concept is much larger than that.

Another familiar dimension of justice is that of fairness. It seems that we are all born with an innate sense of fairness. You can observe this quality in children from the earliest age. They are very sensitive to unfairness, especially when it relates to the relative portions of sweets that are allocated to siblings. 'It's not fair!' is a common heart-felt cry from a child who believes that he or she is the victim of injustice.

When one looks closer at the root word 'just', one finds definitions such as equitable, deserved, well-grounded, even-handed. Justice relates to the allocation of rewards and punishments as well as fairness. One of the most familiar representations of justice is a set of scales weighing the balance and thus an important aspect of justice is finding the right measure or balance.

Plato held that justice was one of the four cardinal virtues and explored in his dialogues its application in life. His best known work, *The Republic*, is dedicated to determining the true meaning of justice. Here and elsewhere Plato observed that justice means 'no excess': the right measure obtains in all situations and at all times.

PRINCIPLES AND VALUES AT WORK

He describes it as a principle of harmony, enabling people to dwell together, the civilizer of humanity and the essential virtue of the state, in which every constitution must share. He argues that the just person is happy and that there is no escape for the unjust.

Another major influence on our understanding of justice comes from Justinian, the emperor who embedded in Roman law the concept that:

> Justice consists in the constant will to render to every man
> his due.
>
> Justinian, *Codex Justinianus*

But what is meant by 'due'? It may be understood in terms of benefits or rewards, and retribution or punishments. It may refer to that which is correct, exactly right for the situation or it may refer to getting or providing just what is needed.

As with all the virtues it relates both to an inner state and to a social dimension governing our relationships with others. What does justice mean in a business context? A business is a social institution and as such requires laws and rules that regulate behaviour. The primary aspects of justice that require the attention of moral managers are fairness and equity.

The company needs to be fair to its employees. This relates to the entire range of employment policies, including pay, promotion, holidays, maternity leave, sickness, and so on. The list is long. In many of these areas there are government regulations which regulate companies' activities. This is only necessary because employers have been unjust in the past. Where there is injustice, or perceived injustice, poor relations between employers and employees are the result, and business suffers a loss of profits while employees suffer loss of wages, and unhappiness is the result all round.

This requirement for the company to be fair is reciprocated. The employees need to be fair to their employer, delivering a full measure of work for the compensation they receive, not abusing trust by helping themselves to company property or cheating on their expenses. It is fair for the company to require a full day's work, and sometimes more if the need arises, but not fair to expect continual long hours that allow the employees no time for their families and private activities. It is fair to expect employees to observe the company policies and procedures, not to strike for frivolous reasons, or at an individual level to take sick leave when they are not ill.

The company needs to be fair to its customers, delivering a valuable product or service, on time and for a fair price. When it makes a mistake it needs to be fair about rectifying it as quickly and fully as it can. The customers need to be fair by not making unreasonable requests of the company and by paying their bills on time. All companies are customers of their suppliers, so these obligations of fairness rest with them in that role too. Far too many large companies treat their suppliers as free sources of finance by delaying their payments. The government has legislated to outlaw this practice but to little avail; suppliers are understandably loath to take a big customer to court or even to threaten to do so. This excessive use of commercial power by the strong against the weak is injustice, and it acts as a blight on the economy. Just actions always promote economic activity and unjust ones always damage it.

The company needs to be fair to its investors. This means being open and transparent in its reporting, and paying its executives reasonably. There are many companies where the executives ignore this principle of fairness. For instance in the USA, the ratio of the pay of the CEO to that of a production worker has long been a gauge of compensation equity within a company. As recently as ten years ago one might have expected that if a factory worker or clerk was paid $20–30,000 per year (roughly £15–20,000 per year) then the CEO might be paid twenty to thirty times that or $450–500,000 (£300–400,000) which might seem excessive to some, but was nevertheless generally accepted. However, in 2004, the ratio of the average CEO's pay to that of production workers at 367 top US corporations reached 431 to 1 (Bloxham and Nash, 2005).

In 2004 the average pay packages for CEOs at big US companies was $10m, up thirteen per cent on 2003 levels (Myers, 2005). Such excessive payments to those at the top are fair neither to investors nor to employees.

The excess in terms of executive compensation is not the only issue where companies are not being fair to their investors. Another sensitive issue is the failure to disclose fully and accurately what is happening in the boardroom. Christopher Cox, chairman of the US Securities and Exchange Commission, (SEC) was reported as saying:

> Over time, the prevalent forms of compensation have migrated away from what is transparent to what is opaque. In many cases, the lion's share of an executive's compensation might come in forms that almost entirely elude disclosure. That clearly needs to be addressed.
>
> Cox, 2005

A number of companies in the United Kingdom, particularly but not only in the financial sector, are moving in the same direction.

A company needs to be fair to its community and the nation by paying proper taxes, submitting financial reports according to regulation, caring for the environment in its production and other processes. It needs to recognize that its activities are an important part of the social fabric of the communities in which it operates, and that if for instance it has to reduce employment due to adverse circumstances, it needs to take every possible step to minimize the impact of such actions. That is justice, and it needs to be accompanied by truthful, open communication as a friend who is an American banker discovered:

> My bank decided to accept an offer for the takeover of its business by another bank. This would have a dramatic impact on all staff and cause concerns for job security, severance, retirement and benefits. This presented a challenge to senior officers who had to manage staff with such concerns, and at the same time continue to ensure the effective operation of the bank through the productive efforts of everyone.
>
> As the President and COO, I called a meeting of senior management prior to the announcement of the sale. We reviewed our management culture, which included articulating the reasons for our success. We decided to reaffirm our management principles and to keep them in the forefront of our daily activities. In particular we decided that the most important aspect of the successful completion of the merger would be the recognition of employee concerns and their honest and sincere resolution.

Prior to the public announcement of the merger we conducted various meetings with staff to inform them of the transaction. Adhering to the principle of openness, we provided staff with all the information we had at that time. We further promised to keep all staff in the loop with regular meetings, a newsletter, and immediate dissemination of announcements.

If individual concerns were expressed by employees, our personnel department was instructed to listen to each concern and either provide an answer or inform the employee that an answer would be obtained from the acquiring bank as soon as possible. In many cases the senior officer was involved with this process to ensure compliance with our goal of providing an honest and sincere response.

In the end we realized that providing honest and sincere communication allayed the fears and concerns of employees. It became evident to all the senior officers that we continued to earn the respect and trust of the employees as we worked our way through the merger process.

We set out in Chapter Five a road map showing how an organization can attain long term sustainable profits by working to principles, by being virtuous. If the guiding principles of justice, fairness and equity are consistently applied, then an atmosphere of confidence and trust will be created, one which appeals to our innate sense of justice. The corollary is also true. If the excesses that are becoming all too common in business today are allowed to continue, then an atmosphere of doubt and mistrust will manifest, resulting in frustration, anger and a demotivated work force.

Confucius had some good advice for CEOs and directors:

> If you govern the people by laws, and keep them in order by penalties, they will avoid the penalties, yet lose their sense of shame. But if you govern them by your moral excellence, and keep them in order by your dutiful conduct, they will retain their sense of shame, and also live up to this standard.
>
> Confucius, *Analects,* 1971 edn.

Good and just policies and rules, which are fair to all, need to be established in a company by the executives, who need to apply these policies and rules fairly, to themselves as well as to everyone else. It is the responsibility of the executives to look after their people and to see that policies are for the benefit of all. That is fair.

One of Chris's clients relates two experiences relating to justice at work:

> 'My brother-in-law, a priest and successful entrepreneur, told me when I was young and green in business about the distinction between moral purity and moral effectiveness. Moral purity is seeing something a bit smelly, drawing attention to the smell and passing by on the other side so as not to be contaminated by it. Moral effectiveness is seeing something a bit smelly, grabbing a shovel and jumping in to do something about it. Both routes are perfectly moral: I have no doubt that I prefer effectiveness.
>
> 'A Japanese employer became concerned when I refused point blank, on two separate occasions, to fire British executives when there was no performance reason for the decisions, just prejudice. It required active intervention over

time to preserve their positions. Some time later we undertook a redundancy programme which was clearly targeted at Western staff and omitting any locally-employed Japanese staff. I took a stand on this, which became a *cause célèbre*, and resulted in at least one such long-protected person losing his (very obviously redundant) job alongside British staff.'

His second experience concerns whistle-blowing, or what he describes as 'not rolling over and playing dead':

'Many people have really devastating decisions to make about whistle blowing: I have never been in such a lonely position. The closest was an incident when I was running an Asian state-owned bank. After just two weeks, with several key staff on holiday, a senior manager came to my office to show me a telex from an African affiliate bank paying a million dollars to his personal account. "Don't worry, it's quite usual," he told me. "The real payee is a general from that country and his account is one digit different. I just thought you'd like to know so you won't be worried about it."

'What to do?

'I called my Head of Internal Audit and asked for an immediate audit of all accounts to find out how widespread the practice was and what other incidents I needed to be aware of. I also called my Compliance Head, a former Bank of England official, to establish the legal position. His advice was absolutely clear. "Call the regulator (the Financial Services Authority) and the City of London Police Anti Money-Laundering line – at once. Then call Head Office."

The consequences of this were immediate, serious and career-defining for me. Head Office never forgave me, nor did the Asian staff in London. The authorities took a tough line but were in no doubt that I was right, and I have never for a second regretted the decision.'

Freedom

Freedom is very closely related to justice. One of the hallmarks of our democratic society is the high value placed upon freedom, another of the cardinal virtues supported by all the major spiritual traditions.

Freedom does not mean licence for individuals to do and say exactly as they please. With freedom come duties and responsibilities. To exercise our responsibilities requires a degree of discipline. There are countless distractions and temptations that draw us away from our duty and towards other paths, such as the pleasurable or the familiar. In most cases these paths divert us from our duty.

One of the most striking paradoxes of our free and liberal society is that the best way to safeguard our freedom is to abide by our values and related disciplines. Historically in Europe it has been the Judaeo-Christian values that have guided society and its leaders, such as respect for the law, for individual freedoms, and proper care for the disadvantaged. If we lose touch with these values then we shall find ourselves eroding the foundations on which freedom rests rather than increasing liberty.

In the United Kingdom we enjoy a large measure of political freedom. We are free to think and say what we please within the bounds set by the law. We cannot make racist statements or slander another, but we are free from the need to guard our speech lest we be overhead by some spy or secret policeman. We also enjoy a measure of economic freedom, in that most of us have enough money to live a decent life. However many people do not experience that freedom and regard themselves as slaves to their mortgage, their credit card debts or their job. This leads to a striving for wealth in the belief that it will deliver freedom, despite the evidence that most of those with much wealth not only appear to work such long hours that they have little time to enjoy their wealth but, more importantly, are continually striving for more. There is never enough money, and when money loses its meaning, because the individual has so much, then the desire typically turns to power. Evidently true freedom does not lie in that direction.

One of the most prevalent desires today is for independence. This is seen as another expression of freedom. There are actually two kinds of independence and one of them is damaging to your health. The negative version sounds like this:

> 'I do not want to be dependent upon anyone or anything. I want to be free to do what I want, when I want with no limitations. I am a free agent and as a result am not willing to enter into relationships where my commitments are dependent on someone else.'

Such an approach to independence is self-centred and leads to isolation, not independence. The other approach is to recognize that in truth we are all completely inter-dependent. Whatever we do affects others for better or worse. Every action you take affects someone else. For instance if you serve another then they appreciate it and are more likely to serve someone else in their turn. If you serve poorly, or withhold service, then the other person is likely to be upset and that will colour their relations with others as well as you. It is the same with families, communities, companies and nations.

However this does not mean that independence is unattainable. What needs to be recognized is what freedom and independence really mean. Earning money is fine. Attaining great wealth is fine. Success is fine. The important thing is not to be attached to the money, wealth or success, not to be dependent upon them, for they will surely pass. If there is no attachment to the wealth, then one can be free to enjoy it. If one is free from the attachment to success, then one can be free from the inevitable attachment to failure and the mental pain it brings, for nobody enjoys only success.

If you act in this way, it is not the results that are important but rather the intention behind the action and the way the action is executed. Thus you are not dependent on the praise or on avoiding the censure of another for your satisfaction. This approach leads to self-reliance. It gives a great self-confidence, a natural state which is not dependent on any external things to sustain it. You are able to treat 'success and failure, those two impostors, just the same'.

Then you may recognize the interdependence that naturally exists between all people. There is a natural ease in the company of others, a natural willingness to give without being dependent on a reward. This generosity is usually returned by a mutual concern and commitment from others. This form of independence is real freedom and leads to a sense of unity with those with whom you work.

A human being, because of his or her unique intellectual and emotional capacities, has the ability and the freedom to choose. When we do not have the strength to choose that which we know to be true, then we are no longer availing ourselves of our natural freedom. We are bound. Habitual thoughts and actions bind us. When we come under the sway of habit we are not free. It is a useful exercise to observe your individual patterns of thought to see whether you are free or whether your responses are limited to a narrow range of options governed by your past experience and the ideas prevalent in society at the time.

For example, your habitual desire for money or success may mean that a choice is presented which may lead to your lying or cheating in order to be successful. Are you then free to choose what you know is right or are the internal pressures so great that you are prepared to sacrifice your freedom for the sake of material gain? Each of us must test ourselves in practice to see where we stand on this issue.

One person who was tested and found wanting was Scott Sullivan, previously the Chief Financial Officer for WorldCom, who co-operated with the CEO, Bernie Ebbers in perpetrating the largest accounting fraud in US history. At his trial Sullivan acknowledged his crime:

> 'Every day I regret what happened at WorldCom. I violated the trust placed in me. My actions were inexcusable. I chose the wrong road and in face of intense pressure I turned away from truth.'
>
> (quoted in Bayot, 2005)

Sullivan was given a light sentence of five years for co-operating with the authorities but Ebbers, who remained unrepentant, was sentenced to twenty-five years in prison: a strong signal that corporate crime will be punished.

We shall now discuss briefly the eight foundational values, which when put into practice in a business, become its virtues.

Courage

Courage, according to Aristotle, holds the middle ground between cowardice and foolhardiness. Courage is what enables us to do what we know is right. Therefore without courage there can be no justice. Wisdom and courage are closely related. Wisdom is knowing what is good and courage is doing what is good. Thus courage depends on wisdom as its guide, but it is also a necessary part of wisdom and virtue. Without courage, wisdom and virtue would be ineffective and hypocritical. However, wisdom and virtue are effective, because courage is in fact a necessary part of them.

Both Confucius and Plato considered courage as a vital aspect of the whole person.

> Holding fast to one's own roots is the foundation of courage.
>
> To see what is right and not do it is cowardice.
>
> Confucius, *Analects*, 1971 edn.
>
> Those who know how to deal well with the terrors and dangers are courageous and those who are mistaken in this are cowards.
>
> Plato, *Republic*

To speak the truth often requires courage, especially if it must be spoken in a hostile environment. A large organization with many power groups can be such an environment. It takes courage to admit a mistake or to turn down business because one believes that a commitment could not be met. It takes courage to speak out against a policy or the actions of superiors that are damaging to the organization. To be courageous is to be committed and determined. Chris recalls just such a situation.

> As the manager of a business unit serving the finance sector, I was bidding to a number of banks for the bespoke development of systems to provide high value payments. All the banks had both common business and technical requirements and individual ones. They all had to meet the same deadline to go live with their systems. We had a limited supply of the skills relating to the common aspects. After much sales effort, we succeeded in winning three contracts for different banks. We still had an outstanding offer to a fourth. This bank then indicated to me that we were their preferred supplier. I knew that we could deliver three systems, but to try to deliver four would put all four at risk of failure. However I was under strong pressure from senior management to accept the fourth contract, because it represented a substantial revenue opportunity. I stuck to my decision and, without formally turning the business down, ensured that the fourth bank was aware of the risks involved. They selected another supplier and we delivered our three contracts on time.

Another aspect of courage is sticking to one's values, as one of our colleagues discovered:

> 'I was offered a position in the large consulting company I worked for by a general manager whose values were not in line with mine. I did not accept the offer. What followed was being excluded from communication, from meetings and

being restricted in terms of my function. This was painful in the beginning, but later on I was happy that I had stuck to my values, because it became clear to me that my vocation was to go in a different direction in my profession.

'Later as an independent consultant I was offered a contract to give coaching lessons in economics to a master craftsman. My professional goal was to coach in terms of human resources and work–life balance. At that time I did not have any other contracts and was short of money. I accepted the contract and felt that I had betrayed myself: following the need for income instead of following my professional goal. But what I found over time was that the master craftsman needed coaching on work–life balance and a personal value system more than understanding economics. I learned that I need to keep my professional goals in my heart, when due to the needs of the moment, I undertake other consulting assignments. Two years later I was asked by the same company to coach four other managers.'

Loyalty

To be loyal means to be true or faithful to one's duty. This may be to one's family, company, sovereign, nation, religion, etc. Loyalty properly given works both ways. In a business context, the employee is loyal to the company and the company to the employee.

Both are less in evidence than they used to be. Employment with many companies used to mean a job for life, and the care and support offered by the company for many aspects of their employees' lives encouraged the development of a sense of loyalty in return. Today people are more flexible, expecting to work for a number of employers during their career, while in many industries managers are quick to resort to redundancies when times are hard. The current emphasis by employees on personal freedom and flexibility and the unwillingness of companies to take on certain responsibilities have undermined the sense of company loyalty. But it is not absent and there are many examples of strong loyalty in both directions. Loyalty is still valued and ignoring it can lead to trouble.

Chris recalls a time when his loyalty was put to the test:

> I had not long taken over responsibility for a software development business that had been losing money. Morale was poor and the outlook was bleak. We started to take steps to redress the situation, sales improved and things were on the mend. Then I was approached by an old friend and colleague who had set up his own business and was doing very well. As he was a visionary rather than a manager, he recognised the need for someone to run his business and he offered me the role of Managing Director. I admired him and thought his product had enormous potential. It was a very attractive opportunity but I felt that I could not let my people down by leaving them when there was still so much to do to turn the business round. I declined the offer and stayed. Interestingly, a few years later my friend found himself in a similar situation and took the same decision.

What can and should always remain is loyalty to one's values, to one's principles.

Magnanimity

This is a word that is falling out of use. In fact when presenting an introductory course in Philosophy to a group of reasonably well-educated, intelligent people, one twenty-something young lady asked what the word meant. From the looks of some others in the class, she was not the only one who did not know.

Sir Charles (C. P.) Snow, the author, spoke on magnanimity at his induction ceremony as Rector of St Andrews University in 1962. He said:

> The virtue consists, first, of seeing oneself and another person as both really are: for there is no virtue without clear sight. And then exerting oneself to see the best in the other person and trying to get the best out of him. Which means, of course, that in the process one is trying to get the best out of oneself.
>
> Snow, 1962.

This definition brings out the nobility that is embodied in the word, which comes from *magnus*, great, noble + *animus*, mind: noble minded. Its more common meaning of generous is also obvious in Snow's definition which highlights how in giving to another we are also beneficiaries.

A magnanimous person is benevolent and friendly. When this quality manifests in the managers of a business, a cohesiveness and positive atmosphere arises, one in which the needs of others are of continual concern. This is first directed to fellow employees and then to customers, the community and on out. *Magnus* can be very large.

One way in which magnanimity can manifest is through the

practice of unselfishness. Chris writes of his experience of seeking to build these virtues into the fabric of the company.

> When we started Charteris we adopted a business model whereby the directors and business consultants were paid a low salary but a substantial proportion of the fees that the company invoiced to clients for their work. This had a number of advantages. It kept the company's overheads low, it shared risk with the staff since they were paid little if they were not on charge to a client, and it enabled good consultants to earn more than they would have done on a salary-based model. It also helped to ensure that they delivered high quality work, as their income depends on the clients settling their bills. It has worked very well. However the model also carries the risk that by focusing the consultants' attention on their own fee paid work, it could lead to selfishness. They do not receive any financial reward for selling the services of their colleagues. We recognised this risk and determined that we would make unselfishness a key principle and that we as directors would set the example. If we spot an opportunity for a colleague, we are serving the client by bringing it to his attention and introducing the colleague who can help him. We expect no more than a 'Thank you' in return. No obligation is created that the colleague will return the compliment, but of course they would naturally do so when they can. As we explain to potential recruits when they ask about this aspect, unselfishness works and so does selfishness, but they produce different results.

Patience

Patience is the calm endurance of anything that may cause pain, whether physical, mental or emotional. It involves being steadfast and persistent. This requires an inner stillness and strength, one which can withstand the distractions and provocations that come from within and without.

In business today there is great pressure on short term performance. A manager is continually evaluated on a monthly, quarterly and yearly basis to make sure that the predicted results are delivered. This is normally intended to create pressure and usually does. This pressure is especially stressful for publicly listed companies where senior managers often have one eye on the business and the other on the share price. In this tense atmosphere, patience is in short supply. Although it is entirely appropriate to measure and judge by results, this focus on short term results may not be best for business in the long run.

Paul recalls:

> A conversation I had in the late 1960s with a manager from a Japanese computer firm has remained for me an indicator of the value of patience. He said to me that they had a twenty-year plan to design, build and bring to market the largest and fastest super-computer. Given that the likes of IBM, Univac, Burroughs and my company Control Data had a substantial lead in this market, I questioned whether such an objective was practical. His calm response was that they have a great deal of patience and that western companies rarely think more than three years ahead in their planning. It is not surprising that by the late 1980s Fujitsu had

produced the fastest super-computer of the day and that Control Data, Univac and Burroughs were out of business, while IBM was focusing on its services business.

Respect

Respect is deference, esteem or honour given to another. These are unfashionable concepts but nevertheless valid in business. Respect is a virtue much prized and easily practised in a business environment.

There are many ways in which respect can be shown including common courtesy. Courtesy in some Eastern cultures has been developed to a fine art while in the West it seems that it is not observed with such rigour as in the past.

> Courtesy is the most precious of jewels. The beauty that is
> not perfected by courtesy is like a garden without a flower.
>
> *Buddhacharita*, cit. in The Eternal Wisdom, 1995

It is a sign of respect when an effort is made to understand and appreciate the values of another culture in which one is doing business, an important consideration in a global business climate.

At an even finer level, respect is expressed when your actions are based on the principle of doing onto others as you would have them do unto you, which as we have noted, is universal in its scope. Another equally fine reason for respect to be offered is in the full belief that to 'love thy neighbour as thyself' is the true basis for all relationships.

The foundation of respect for others is of course self-respect. This comes first and is necessary if sincere respect is to be offered to others. The secret is to respect everyone equally, regardless of their rank or position. Then the respect is automatically returned. When you act in this way you find that your self-respect increases too. Sadly the corollary is true too. If people are not respected then they lose their self-respect.

Above all, respect thyself.

Pythagoras, *Golden Verses of Pythagoras*

With respect comes freedom, as one of our friends describes:

'I was a senior manager of a major telecommunications company. At one point I was in charge of more than 200 people with a multi-million pound budget.

'Good communications are vital for maintaining trust. My door was always open for anyone in the department. They were encouraged to be open and I always tried to be straight and direct in my responses.

'One aspect of our meetings that was important was that for any requests for resources or finance, I would only accept the truth. I discouraged the common practice of exaggerating the need in order to negotiate later. People responded very well to this simple approach. It made them feel free to speak.

'There was never any gender or race discrimination. I respected every person as a member of the team and this became the guiding principle for all members.

'The staff were trusted and given numerous freedoms. For example, during the Christmas period they were given extended lunch periods to do shopping or if they needed extra time to sort out domestic issues, it was assumed that they would provide cover for their work and make up the time when needed in the future. They responded positively to such freedoms by acting very responsibly.

'On one occasion when the demand arose for a new departmental Health and Safety programme, I appointed a lady who had no specific experience but was an excellent administrator. I told her that I could trust her and that she had the freedom to examine what was required and to implement a solution. She performed the task in an efficient and creative manner.

'When trust was violated I would listen very carefully to the arguments. The aim was to be able to make a reasonable response. The employee was usually given the benefit of doubt for which they were very grateful.

'I believe that it is important for managers to listen both to their people and to their inner voice so that the true knowledge can arise to meet the need.'

Responsibility

The word literally means 'the ability to respond'. Someone who is responsible is morally accountable for his actions, reliable, of good repute, trustworthy. This clearly applies to individuals. People are given responsibilities when they have shown that they are trustworthy. They are then judged on how well they can be depended upon to continue to fulfil their obligations. Quite properly, a responsible person is highly valued in business.

Responsible companies are also highly valued.

Forty-four per cent of the British public believe it is very important that a company shows a high degree of social

responsibility when they buy that company's product.
Fifty-eight per cent of the general public across Europe feel
that industry and commerce do not pay enough attention to
their social and environmental responsibilities.

Little, 2003

The lack of trust in business that we have highlighted is becoming of great concern to many companies, especially those offering consumer products where reputation and brand are among their most valuable assets. For example, it is estimated that ninety-six per cent of Coca Cola's value comprises intangibles: reputation, knowledge and brand (Blunden, 2004). When that company suffered from scandal in March 2004 over its marketing of bottled tap water, treated so as to contain bromate, a carcinogen and branded as Dasani, the damage to its reputation far exceeded the cost of wasted production, advertising, and packaging.

However when companies do suffer from events which damage their reputation, they can recover through slowly working to mend that reputation. This requires many of the other virtues – patience, temperance, tolerance of the views of those who oppose or attack them, courage and vitally, dedication to the truth.

One of our friends describes his experience of taking his responsibility seriously:

'An entrepreneur built up a group of companies in the environmental industry. I was hired as Chief Operating Officer (COO) for these companies to provide the transition to a more formal organization.

'The existing organization was conditioned to cut corners on most things and was not cognizant of the current or evolving environmental regulations. The treatment of hazardous waste is time consuming and expensive if done properly. It is tempting to take shortcuts to achieve lower costs rather than applying proper treatment. It is essential to install and enforce the controls to assure compliance with the laws.

'There was an attitude that if politicians received contributions they would assist in awarding contracts and keeping the regulatory agencies from investigating the company.

'The informal organization functioned to circumvent management controls and an operating mantra was "Do what the owner wants". It was difficult to prove that people were doing what he wanted, whether or not it was proper, but they were.

'As COO, I was the responsible person to sign all legal documents relating to environmental compliance as well as other major documents, such as merger or acquisition papers. The owner signed very few legal documents, but controlled the content of all of them.

'I had many discussions with the owner on this and other management topics but to no avail. I never saw any actual illegal activity nor was ever pressured to perform an illegal or unethical action. However, there was an atmosphere that felt very uncomfortable, as if I was just on the outside of unsavoury operations. I imagined a possible situation in which I would be trying to defend myself for actions that I was not aware had happened yet had certified that they could not have taken place. I was the responsible person! I resigned after about a year in the position.

A postscript: ten years later the general manager of one of the companies that I had managed was sent to prison for an environmental infraction that happened while he was running that operation.'

Temperance

In modern usage temperance has taken on its secondary meaning of abstinence from alcohol, but as one of the cardinal virtues it means moderation and self-restraint in action of any kind, including the expression of opinions. This is a virtue to practise in business. It requires that you be open-minded, for instance in a meeting, respecting the positions which others take and seeking common ground.

Temperance requires discrimination and discipline consistently applied. When such self-restraint is practised for a sufficient time, it becomes natural and the struggle goes out of it. It is especially important that leaders set a good example in applying proper measure.

> When rulers love to observe the rules of propriety, the people respond readily to the calls on them for service.
>
> Confucius, *Analects*, 1971 edn.

It seems the real challenge for business leaders today is to find the right measure. The problem in general is not earning enough to survive, it is knowing what is enough. We need to learn to manage in a world where excess seems to be the rule, rather than the exception. Temperance is well described in the wise aphorism offered by Plato: 'Nothing to excess' (Plato, *Republic*).

Tolerance

The virtue of tolerance embraces patience with or indulgence towards the opinions or practices of others, and freedom from bigotry and undue severity in judging their conduct. It requires forbearance. In business one comes up against all sorts of opinions, attitudes and behaviour. People in a company have not necessarily come together because they share opinions and beliefs but rather because they can together provide a product or service that the market wants. This very heterogeneity may be a real advantage in making up teams to fulfil particular roles, but for those teams to be effective, people need to practise tolerance.

Armed with these virtues, the moral manager is in a position to give attention to service, the heart of any business. That is the topic of our next chapter.

CHAPTER 9 - SERVICE, THE HEART

A ction, which includes all mental as well as physical activity, is obviously an integral part of life. As human beings we cannot refrain from action. Any action, including activities that we describe as service, involves:

● an **actor** – you or your company;

● the **action** – the execution of the activity;

● the **results** of the action.

For the purposes of our investigation into the nature and quality of business service we shall consider one important aspect of each of these three elements:

● the **intention** of the actor;

● the **attention** with which the action is carried out;

● the **retention** or claim that is put on the results of the action.

We shall examine each of these in turn.

Intention

The intention is the **motive** behind the action. It provides the **emotional power** behind the action. It includes the object of the action, i.e. to what or to whom the action is **dedicated**.

Football players in a World Cup competition or Olympic athletes may compete for the sake of their country, for their fellow players, for their own sake or for the sake of the game itself. Employees may work for a wage packet, in order fully to express their talents, or as part of a team providing a valuable service. A company may be dedicated to providing a good service for a fair

OF BUSINESS

return or it may be in business to maximize profit at any cost. These examples show how our intentions influence the way we conduct business.

Two actions may on the surface appear to be the same. Take two sales representatives who each achieve the same sales value in a year. Performance on the surface is the same but one would have to look deeper to ascertain the motivation for each. If the values differ then the actions will be powered by different energies. Consequently there will be qualitative difference in the results.

If one is driven solely by how much money is made, then one is more likely to do or say anything needed to get the business. The focus is on the sale and not necessarily the quality of the product or service delivered nor whether it benefits the customer. As soon as the sale is completed a salesperson motivated by cash is off for the next deal.

The other salesperson may be motivated by a strong desire to provide a real solution to a customer's needs while earning a reasonable profit for the organization and a commensurate commission. He or she may well achieve more than making the sales quota. For example, the good service provided is likely to enhance the reputation of the company and make it more likely that additional business will be forthcoming from the customer for many years to come.

Attention

A diagram that we have found useful in understanding and explaining the activities involved in meeting the needs of a customer is as follows:

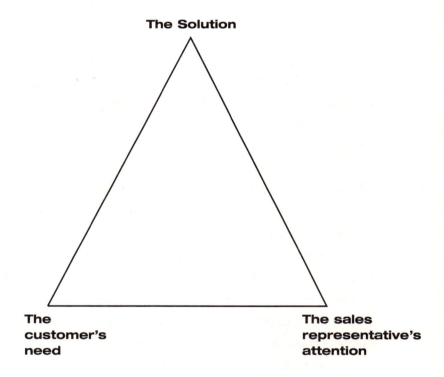

The Solution

The customer's need

The sales representative's attention

Let us first look at the application of attention from the perspective of the sales representative. He or she must have a clear, detailed and objective view of the capabilities of his or her own company, then look with full attention at the prospective customer's situation to gain an understanding of their specific need. In some cases this need may not yet have been fully formulated by the customer. When both the capabilities and the need are seen clearly, good judgements can be made about whether the company can be of service and, if so, how its product or service will satisfy the need.

What often happens is that the sales representative's attention is distracted and the contact with the prospect is dominated by pre-conceptions, assumptions and fixed ideas on the solution. Often the ideas are based on past experience or future expectations and not on what is being presented now by the particular person or situation.

This lack of complete attention in the moment often gets in the way of satisfying the internal needs of a company too. For example, when you meet your boss, a package of ideas, associations and emotions can crowd the show and colour just how you react in the moment. The same might apply when you are meeting those whom you manage. Often the influence of the past or the anticipation of the future are so strong that we do not hear or see what is actually going on in the moment.

The power of careful attention is most obvious when one is watching a fine artist or craftsman at work. These examples of full attention are wonderful to watch. They bring joy to the observer and result in a fine product that continues to manifest this joy. This same joy can be tasted in a business context too. To be there, in the moment, is the key.

Retention

Retention in this context refers to the claims that we put on an action. Often our primary concern is for my results, my performance, my recognition. We all like our actions to have 'good' results. During our days at school, achieving the highest exam results, winning at sports, passing music or ballet exams consumed a great deal of our energies. Then we became concerned with results of getting a good degree, a good job with an attractive compensation package, loaded with perks; we become interested in the increasing value of our house, the make, model and registration date of our car, and so on. All these are quantitative measures of success, all easily comparable against others', resulting in a highly competitive environment.

What is common in these examples is that the success or failure is fully attributed to the individual, typically 'me'. A claim is made on the result and as a consequence, a person's state of mind and being is affected by the result. The only way out is not to identify with the result.

This is not so easy. Are there many occasions in your life when you have been neutral about winning or succeeding? When was the last time you were happy to lose? When was the last time you played a game for the fun of it without worrying how well you were performing or whether you won or lost? Do you believe that losing make you less of a person?

This story summarizes Chris's experience:

> A few years ago I was leading the sales campaign for a big government consulting engagement. I met a senior partner in my firm on the platform as we waited for our trains to go home. He was personally interested in this proposal. 'We must win this job, Chris,' he said. I said I was putting my all into the proposal, as were my team and that we would work as hard as was necessary to ensure that it was a good proposal. 'But whether we win or lose,' I said, 'is secondary. If we win, that will be good; if we lose, then we just move on. I make a practice of not wanting to win, but just doing my

best. That way, I don't get the euphoria of winning but I don't have to suffer the misery of losing.' His reaction suggested he thought I was slightly mad, so I persisted. 'How long does the pleasure of winning last?' I asked. 'Oh, a few minutes' he said. 'And the pain of losing?' 'Days or weeks,' was his reply. 'You can either have both or neither,' I concluded as we boarded the train, 'but not one without the other.'

It is the same with praise. How often have you observed in yourself and others the generous giving of praise to others, giving credit where it is due? If someone compliments you on the actions of your team, do you pass it on to the team members, or do you take the credit yourself? Have you found yourself at times envious of the success of others? Does the success of others make you feel less by comparison? All of these reactions are driven by the attachment to the result of the action – retaining too much for me. The more examples there are of people sharing praise and recognition with others, the easier it will be for everyone in an organisation to let go of such an attachment.

The giving of service

We speak in everyday English of giving service. It is well within our own experience that in giving the giver receives as well as the recipient. One version of this principle, enunciated in many faiths is, 'In giving, we receive'. Even stronger but equally common is the principle that 'it is more blessed to give than to receive.' (e.g. Acts 20:35)

It is worth considering why this is true. A mother asks for nothing in return for the service given to her family but is blessed through her actions by having a happy family. The blessing comes in the form of a deeply felt and natural happiness which is the lawful result of someone acting in accordance with her true nature. The premise is that giving, and by extension giving service, is natural for the human being. Why then is there apparently so much more taking than giving, particularly in business?

When we refuse to serve or serve only to get something in return, the benefits are reduced or even eliminated for both receiver and giver. We cover over our true nature, we ignore it and the price paid is access only to a lesser happiness or even sorrow.

Service, both given and received, is necessary for our very survival. Just consider all the services upon which you and your business depend for your existence. You could not survive in society unless food was produced, brought to shops and offered for sale. You could not keep warm unless electricity and gas were provided by utility companies. You could not move about unless roads were maintained, public transport operated, and so on. We may imagine that we are independent individuals, but in fact we are highly dependent on each other for the provision of a wide range of services.

So does this mean that we are advocating not charging for the services we render in a business context? Are businesses then charities? Certainly not. Businesses have to generate revenue and make a profit in order to attract investment and indeed to survive. Therefore they must sell products and/or services and must charge a proper price for what they do. It is entirely appropriate, essential in most cases, that the service be paid for. However, when you are giving service in the course of your business activity, you should be giving it. The payment comes later. It is linked in an obvious way to the service – the service is what the payment is for. But if your attention is on what you will get paid rather than on the giving of the service, on the retention, then the service will be half-hearted and the customer will always notice. Give service fully and you will in fact be rewarded for it. That is the way it works.

A larger view of service

We need to open up our view of service so we can make some assessment of the quality of service being offered and consider what refinements are possible as a result of seeing the bigger picture.

Here are two larger perspectives:

Teach me, Lord to serve You as You deserve;

To give and not to count the cost;

To fight and not to heed the wounds;

To toil and not seek for rest;

To labour and not to ask for any reward

Save that of knowing that I do Your will.

St Ignatius Loyola, *Prayer for Generosity*

If one could be made to understand that caring for oneself is bondage, while feeding others is freedom, then life would be easy for all.

Shantananda Saraswati, unpublished conversation

Serving feeds and nourishes the giver as well as the receiver. In the context of everyday transactions in the marketplace it is very obvious that excellent service given whole-heartedly not only satisfies the need but can also be a source of inspiration for both parties.

Consider the last time you received really excellent service from someone. What effect did it have on you? Did it not lift your day? You can do the same for others – the opportunity is there all the time.

In order to provide a high quality service, objectivity is required on the part of both parties in the assessment of the need and of the ability of the vendor organization to meet the need effectively. Clarity and realism are necessary, not imaginings, wishful thinking or cleverness. This requirement continues through decision making, commitment and delivery. Through all this, the quality of the final service will depend on:

- the alignment of the motives and values of seller and buyer;
- the degree to which each party is actually in the present moment, that is, attentive to what is happening;
- an honest acknowledgement of their respective contributions.

It is common sense that when customers are well satisfied with the service received, faith and confidence are developed in the provider such that the customers are more likely to come back and buy again even if difficulties are experienced at times. Thus service is a prime indicator of a sustainable business. It helps a business relationship to develop by nourishing and enlivening both parties.

Who serves and who is served?

It is obvious that some people are employed to serve: the customer service agent, the shop assistant, the bank clerk. But what about the salesman, the accounts clerk, the purchasing manager, the human resources manager, the chief executive? Do they serve? Is that what they are there for? If so, whom do they serve?

Our answer is yes in each case. The salesman serves the customer and also his colleagues in design and manufacturing by giving them up-to-date information on what his customers want from the company; he serves the finance function by guiding them to the right people in the customer organization to get the bills paid, and, by making sure that the customer is satisfied with the service he gets, he ensures that there is no reason why the bills are not paid. The accounts clerk serves the salesman and the customer by seeing that the invoices are accurate and timely. He serves the suppliers by paying their bills on time, thus serving the purchasing manager's needs too. He serves management by providing the financial information to enable proper decisions to be made. The purchasing manager serves the rest of the company by ensuring that the materials and tools are there when they are needed, at an appropriate cost, to get the job done. He serves the supplier by stating clearly and objectively what the company needs and when.

It is obvious that the human resources manager serves the needs of all the employees, as well as management, by advising on the impact of policy decisions on the workforce, and by ensuring that the company complies with employment legislation. And the CEO serves the whole company by providing leadership and guidance and by taking timely decisions, and the board and the shareholders by meeting financial, growth and other targets.

Does the secretary serve the director or does the director serve the secretary? In an obvious way the secretary serves the director by typing letters, arranging appointments, and so on. But in a more significant way the director serves the secretary by creating the right working environment, looking after their needs and noticing when the secretary does something well or out of the ordinary. Indeed, true service always flows from the top of the organization downwards, the opposite of what we normally think.

Now what about the customer? Whom does he or she serve? We have already alluded to the customer's responsibility to articulate his needs or desires properly. To do so is to serve the salesman; it means he does not waste his time if he cannot meet the need and helps him to present his product or service in a way that will appeal to the customer. He can also serve the supplier by paying his bills on time and by providing him with appropriate feedback on the product and service being delivered. This was Chris's experience:

> I had a kitchen extension built a couple of years ago. I wrote to a number of local builders with a specification and invited tenders, selected one and negotiated a contract. This was the first time I had dealt with a builder, and after hearing many horror stories, was determined to include penalty clauses and a retention period in the contract. The builder agreed as long as I undertook to pay him weekly. I understood that he needed to pay his tradesmen on that basis and was therefore punctilious about honouring that commitment. He respected that and then, when problems arose which were due to his mistakes or that of his men, he immediately put them right without quibble. In this way the service was mutual, and gradually the trust between us, which had been minimal at the outset, grew. There were problems, as there are in all building contracts, but they were all resolved. It was tough at times, but in retrospect it was a case study in

service and trust and the relationship between them.

Service at the heart of business

Everything we do involves the heart in one way or another, for without the heart there is no life. If our business analogy is to hold, then the heart must permeate all aspects of the business; from birth to death, from the conception of an idea to the final consumption of the end product. Service is part of each stage.

Conception

We have already discussed the idea that the essence of service is the satisfaction of a need. A business begins with the recognition of a need in the market and a vision of how that need may be economically satisfied. The realization may come in a flash or if the need is well known, it may be as a result of research, analysis and experimentation, or a combination of these activities.

In the case of the founding of Paul's company, the idea came as a flash of inspiration, but only after considerable study:

> Our business is training in finance using computer-based self-study products, now called e-learning. I had been working in the field for more than ten years, including a sabbatical year at Oxford University in their Education Studies Department. The aim of the study was to work with teachers, headmasters and educators to learn more about the principles of education so that better decisions could be made about the use of computers to teach.
>
> During these preparatory years I had been asked by the UK Government training agency (the Manpower Services

Commission) to project manage the design and development of e-learning courses in finance for managers of small businesses. I noted during this work how well suited the computer-based methodology was to the teaching of finance, because the computer could provide instant feedback to the student.

Three years later I was demonstrating a new computer-based financial modelling tool to a member of the board of one of the UK's top companies. This well designed tool allowed a manager to input or change any business figure e.g. sales, fixed costs and so on, and immediately see the impact of the decision on the profit, on cash flow, etc. The response of this senior executive to the ease of use of the tool was positive. He said, 'Our managers could learn to use the tool; it is simple enough, but they will not understand what they are looking at.'

In that moment the idea was born. I visualized an e-learning course in practical finance that would help managers better understand how their business decisions affect the financial performance of their company. In that moment my previous experience as to the suitability of computer-based methods for financial learning came together with this clear statement of need and a new service was born, in fact a new company came into being.

Design and development

For a useful product or service to become manifest, more work is required. There are numerous examples of people having blinding revelations as to ways to satisfy recognized needs, but they never go further than an intellectual exercise. The next stage is that the initial idea or conception needs to be refined and a design produced. A development plan is then needed to set out the specific steps to turn the idea into a tangible product or service.

The elements of service that are most evident in this stage are that both the end user and the economic buyer must be kept in mind at all times. If the product is to be a success it must satisfy their needs and so throughout the design and planning processes their needs become the reference points.

Paul continues:

> In our case we recognized that managers, the end users of our product, do not need to know accounting rules and regulations; they need to know the relationships between the elements that contribute to profitability, cash flow and so on, and most importantly how their decisions will impact these key financial measures.
>
> Two other design criteria were established for our products based upon our understanding of the needs. Companies use different financial terminology so we had to make the product flexible enough to allow easy customization to suit specific company needs. Secondly, we needed a product that could easily be translated into other languages as our intended clients, global corporations, would want to have the same understanding among managers in their companies around the world, who would of course speak many different languages.
>
> Once the overall product design was agreed we then had to get down to the details of the internal workings of the

learning program. The needs of the user must be kept in mind at every step along the way. Like a good teacher, the designer must present the subject matter in the most interesting manner to facilitate learning while at the same time anticipating where the student might become confused and need further clarification.

Thus service to the different needs of all the individuals in all our potential clients was in fact the determinant of everything we did in the design and planning process for our new product.

Presentation of the product to the market

The accurate, timely and effective presentation of a product to potential clients is a necessary and useful service. The sales and marketing functions provide the communications link with the market. All too often these functions are given a low priority, de-emphasized or poorly handled, resulting in a great waste of the valuable resources engaged in the development of the product. It becomes a case of unfulfilled potential.

In the case of our e-learning solution, the sales cycle can be longer than a year. During that time a great deal needs to be learned about the client company, its values, processes and procedures. The reason this is important is that the service, the sale, is not complete until both the buyer and the user are satisfied. For instance, we normally sell to HR managers. But the HR manager will typically never use the product; it is other managers in business units around the world who will use it. The sale is only completed once the product has been used by the client's employees. So satisfying one or the other is not enough. We have to ensure that both are content with the product and the service. This requires a well executed implementation plan. The assistance, guidance and support provided to the client by our company is an integral part of our service both before and after the sale. If this aspect of service is not responsive, effective and of high quality, then the client's view of our product will be tainted.

Product packaging

For our products the packaging issues are simple compared to many consumer products but nevertheless getting this decision right depends upon a correct reading of the trends in the market and specific client and user requirements.

For our company, the prevailing technology of the day has been a major determinant of the packaging. Over the seventeen-year product life cycle we have delivered the programme on various computer media e.g. a 5$\frac{1}{4}$-inch floppy disk, 3$\frac{1}{2}$-inch hard disk, CD, later via a network and now online via the Internet using a variety of different versions of Windows. What required most attention was the writing of the user manuals that were part of the disk/CD packaging. It turned out to be a two-three year project of writing material and testing it in the marketplace to make sure that it was clear for our users.

Pricing

How to set the price of your product and service in the market is a crucial issue which requires clear, objective analysis and constant monitoring of user reaction. The aim should be to charge a fair price.

The approach taken by some is to focus on the highest price achievable. There can be a discussion of value in the context of assessing what the competitors are charging and whether we can demonstrate higher value to justify our higher price. Is it fair or even good business to charge the same prices for products in developing countries? It may be better to have local prices for products in countries like South Africa, China and India.

In consumer products where the user has several choices with little to differentiate between products, pricing is often dictated by the competitive situation with little room to manoeuvre. What about in a field such as consulting where it is not always so easy to value the expertise offered? Chris's view:

> In my experience there is no one right price for a service like a consulting study. Factors such as the volume of work, the experience of the consultants, the precision with which the task has been specified, the size of the consulting firm, the length of the project and whether the work is continuous or intermittent all affect the consulting firm's costs and the client's expectations in relation to price. Therefore when I am calculating the fee to charge I have to take all this into account. But equally important is ensuring that, if awarded the contract, we are in a position to deliver a first-class service to the client for a cost which is within his budget and which he will regard as good value. So service to the client is not the only consideration but is ultimately the determining factor.

Contracting/ordering

Paul's experience of this aspect:

> For the early stages of our business we had very little in the
> way of licence agreements and contracts. Over the years it
> became commonplace in the industry to have more detailed
> agreements designed to protect our products from illegal
> copying or use. Agreements with resellers became more
> complex reflecting a business atmosphere that was becoming
> less trusting and more legalistic.

Will this trend continue? What can be done to simplify the
process of doing business? The function of a written contract is to
state clearly the conditions relating to a transaction, particularly
where doubts may arise. The reason for the doubts may range from
the complexity of the agreement to a lack of trust between the parties to a failure by one party to perform its obligations. As the
atmosphere in business today is one in which trust and clarity are
difficult to establish and maintain, the common practice is to have
written agreements.

Because many contracts between a strong party and a weak
party, such as between a big consumer products company or
retailer and an individual consumer, have been unfairly drawn up
by the strong party, it has been felt necessary to pass a body of con-
tract-related legislation in many countries to protect the weaker
party. This is another example of an industry that has been unable
to regulate itself, forcing governments to develop another layer of
laws. In these cases the laws override the contractual terms. All this
adds yet more complexity, cost and time to the process of contracting for business.

Chris's company took a different approach:

> My consulting company employs many associates, typically people who have a particular skill that our own team does not have, to complement our skills and deliver a complete service to our clients. We have developed a contract to regulate our relationships with our associates. Our guideline in drafting it was that it should be fair and equitable to both parties. New associates don't normally seek to negotiate the terms; they recognize its fairness. This immediately puts our relationship on a good footing, it saves time for both parties and provides a freedom in the relationship.

Product delivery and installation

It is quite common with technology-based products like computers and mobile telephones that beautifully designed and packaged products can be rated very poorly because the user is unable to get them to function easily. This may be due to poor or overly-complex installation and operational instructions, usually those prepared by highly technical people who have little appreciation for those less technically competent. This was the approach of Paul's company :

> In the case of our learning programme we found that two important ingredients were required in the preparation of such instructions; an installation and operation process that was designed to be as simple as possible and a person writing the instructions who was able to describe the process using simple, clear language. Again, thinking about serving the user is key.

Customer support

With the advent of more technological products and the ability to purchase a variety of products and services remotely, via catalogues or online, comes the growing need for customer support. Much of this support is also delivered remotely, via telephone or online. Here again well-designed products and services can be rejected, in this case due to poor customer support.

> In the case of computer-based learning, which is a new field, the importance of providing responsive customer support is especially critical. Any time a person embarks on something new and unfamiliar there is a certain degree of tension. When there is a problem, this tension can easily be aggravated so that small difficulties can cause a serious eruption of emotion.
>
> In an effort to develop a customer support process and system that could be transferred to our distributors in other countries, we kept records of the reasons for support calls and generated a list of frequently asked questions (FAQs) and relevant responses. We also used the profile of problems as feedback into the development group to help guide future product design.

A number of the friends and colleagues who have contributed their experiences wrote of the power of service genuinely given:

> 'I ran a successful real estate company in London for over twenty years. Looking back, I can say that the secret of our success was a mixture of love, knowledge and service.
>
> 'The love was tangible as you walked into the office.

Being a small company, my staff were like my beloved students and members of my family. We all became involved in each other's personal lives and while there was great dedication to the company on their part, there was also great devotion to them on my part. Practical philosophy was central to our daily conversations.

'We also loved our clients: we knew the names of their children, we were genuinely interested in them even if they ended up buying elsewhere. As a result, almost eighty per cent of our business came through client referrals.

'We developed an "A-team" – a network of solicitors, surveyors, mortgage brokers, insurance brokers, handymen, builders whom we liked and who worked like us. We would recommend them to clients when necessary. We had a cardinal rule of never accepting a commission or referral fee from any of these people, so we could continue to serve the clients' best interest. We also never recommended someone we didn't use ourselves. This ensured the success of each transaction and the client could benefit from our years of experience with the members of the A-team. They also gave of their best because of all the repeat business and the trust we had in them.

'We maintained high standards in our knowledge of the property market; the discipline was self-imposed by our staff. We didn't just sell the property and sit back and wait for our commission cheque; we made it our business to be involved in every stage up to the time the transaction was complete and then continued our involvement if it was needed. Our clients were comfortable to call on us at any time and relied on us and treated us as their friends and not just as agents.

'When I started to think of retirement three years ago, my first thought was to sell the business to the highest bidder. Unfortunately, since I was such an integral part of the success of the company, the few buyers who showed an interest insisted on my staying on for at least three more years. I then offered shares to my staff at a hugely discounted rate; they were young and couldn't see the point of paying for something which in the end was dependent on their efforts.

'I finally sat down and thought about what would be best for everyone. My staff wanted to keep their jobs and to continue to build on what they had invested in for several years. I needed to free myself from responsibility for the company and eventually move to the USA. I also needed some income from the company. Our clients needed the continuity of service that they had come to expect from us. So I gave the two individuals who had expressed a strong interest to continue the good work ten per cent each of the shares of the company, a good basic salary and a generous commission structure which took into account their hard work but also factored in the inevitable dip in sales resulting from my departure. I wanted to give them a taste of ownership and a visible proof of the value of their contribution.

'We also settled on a modest consultancy fee for me. Two years have passed; my two wonderful younger partners have held the ship steady, grown in experience and in their team-work together. They are really getting a chance to put into practice all my advice and teaching over the years. I am liberated from the business and have started a new phase of my life. Our clients are as happy as they were while I was around.

'For all this to happen required me to let go of my desire to have things my way and to be satisfied with a modest stipend instead of being able to cash in. My colleagues had to transcend their fear of being left holding the baby.

'I feel good about all the wonderful years during which I worked hard to build up my business and about the freedom I have to have a different life in retirement from it. I feel good that two young people that I loved as my children have inherited a business that will provide them with a good living and the satisfaction of being their own bosses. Unity was served with resulting happiness for all involved.'

Another friend's experience:

'When I joined the recently established UK arm of a large and well-known Finnish office furniture manufacturer in 1982, it was my first direct exposure to the corporate business world. My title was Design Manager and my role was to set up and run the UK design department.

'Within a month or two I was initiated into certain business rituals based on the American model, which the Finns espoused with all the enthusiasm of recent converts. The first of these was the Objective Setting Seminar, an annual two-day jamboree, which was designed to set the company's primary objectives for the coming year and foreseeable future. That it was taken very seriously was borne out by the fact that the Finnish CEO and board directors were all in attendance.

'Following introductory speeches by the CEO and "state-of-play" talks from some of the directors, all personnel were randomly divided into around six teams of eight or so members, one of whom was appointed as the team leader. The teams were then sent off into separate rooms and charged with debating what they saw as the ten key issues for the successful operation of the company over the ensuing period, and list them in order of importance. Towards the end of the second day all teams were brought together again and the team leaders then had to present their findings. Being a new-boy to the game, I was an ordinary team member which allowed me a certain mental freedom in watching events unfold.

'The various team lists in order of one to ten were then amalgamated to produce the final master list which would set the company's operational philosophy for the period to come. I was perplexed to see that placed at number one was the word "profit". At the same time I noticed that sitting at number nine on the list was the word "service". At this point I put up my hand and asked how it was that profit, which is a result, could be, in all reason, placed at number one, while service, which must surely be the primary objective of any right-minded company, was placed at nine? Operationally, how could a company expect the resultant profit without the right priorities of mind-set and function first being in place?

'There was a stunned silence followed by some hasty murmured conferring amongst the directors. Then the CEO went to the whiteboard and very deliberately erased numbers one and nine and reversed their order. From that moment forward service became the key objective. As I said earlier, the Finns take these events seriously. Their business has flourished and is well-regarded in the industry and by their many satisfied customers.'

Here is the experience of a third, a partner in a large accounting firm:

'My firm had developed a simple but profitable service auditing the payroll records of an insurance client's customers. The business grew and the issue arose, how to service this work. The work was rather mundane. Once the initial assignments were complete, the audit programmes specifically written to provide the service, the thrill of taking the product to new clients, once all that was done, the challenge from my perspective was no longer there.

'To keep the flourishing business growing, the need to find someone to drive it forward was becoming pressing. A simple solution then presented itself. The partnership was redirecting (in other words sacking) a number of its older professional managers (good accountants who were not going to make partner). Why not approach one of them who would be prepared to undertake this less than challenging work? One was selected who was in his late forties.

'The service really took off and provided yet another need. The young professional staff engaged in this project were losing interest in the rather mundane work. Solution, simple again: engage retired staff with accounting experience on a part-time basis. This was again new stuff for the partnership. But it worked beautifully. These were experienced staff whose career was over, perhaps a little bored in retirement but who were eager to get one or two days away from their home. They enjoyed doing this type of work. They certainly met our need for professional staff willing to do high quality yet mundane work.

'That was twenty-odd years ago and the business is still growing. I believe the fee income from this simple little business is now several million dollars annually.

'If you focus on a need and respond to it with an open mind, who knows what follows? A few hurdles will present themselves but with simple and practical solutions one can keep focused. In this case it just seemed to flow quite naturally. We were able to meet our business needs, the needs of our client, our staff and the community.'

Summary

The common thread running through this view of service is that focusing on the needs of others, the client and the ultimate user, is fundamental. When this need is kept at the forefront of one's mind then the way to best satisfy the need can become clear and the resources available can be most effectively applied.

You will note that the emphasis has been on the various elements of service and not on profit. It is our contention that by following this road map of beginning with foundation values and concentrating the attention on fine service, profits will follow naturally.

In the next chapter we will look further at the creative impulse which arises to satisfy the needs that have been perceived.

CHAPTER 10 - CREATIVITY AND LOVING

The role of business as proposed is 'the creation of wealth for the benefit of all'. How does one create wealth? What is creativity in business? Do you normally think of business as a creative activity in the same way as poetry, art or music? On the other hand is being creative important in business for an individual, or for a company?

The definition of the word 'create' is to bring into being, to originate and includes such aspects as inventiveness and imagination.

In our Philosophy in Business course we asked the participants what 'creativity in business' meant to them. These are the qualities that emerged:

Original	**Artful**	*Conscious*	**Attentive**
Inventive	*Responsive to the need*		**Free**
In the moment	**Imaginative**		*Visionary*
Ingenious	*Sees the whole*	**Produces beauty**	
Playful	**Detached**		

For descriptions of the creative process we cannot do better than two highly creative individuals, who speak for themselves. First Shakespeare who describes the creative process for the poet:

> And as imagination bodies forth
> The forms of things unknown, the poet's pen

YOUR WORK

Turns them to shapes, and gives to airy nothing

A local habitation and a name.

William Shakespeare, *The Tempest*

Shakespeare is saying that the imagination brings new ideas, as if from nowhere, into being in the mind and then the poet articulates them, that is, gives them a name and form.

This process of an idea emerging from an apparent 'airy nothing' is also called inspiration. The idea seems to arise from within. What are the conditions that are most conducive to this creative impulse?

For this we have some excerpts from a letter from Mozart, considered by many as the greatest creative musical genius.

When I am, as it were, completely myself, entirely alone and of good cheer . . . It is on such occasions that my ideas flow best and most abundantly. Whence and how they come I know not; nor can I force them.

If I continue in this way, it soon occurs to me how I may turn this my dainty morsel to account, so as to make a good dish of it. That is to say, agreeable to the rules of counterpoint, to the peculiarities of various instruments, etc.

All this fires my soul, and provided I am not disturbed my subject enlarges itself becomes methodized and defined and the whole though it be long, stands almost complete and finished in my mind so that I can survey it like a fine picture or beautiful statue at a glance.

> Nor do I hear in my imagination the parts successively,
> but I hear them, as it were, all at once.
>
> What a delight this is, I cannot tell.
>
> Wolfgang Amadeus Mozart, cit. in Mersmann, *Letters*, 1972

Mozart describes the creative process as tapping into an inner knowledge, an intuition. Note the joy that it brings.

Staying with music as the example of the creative process, we can follow the way in which the powers of expression are made manifest in the composer, the musician and the listener.

A composer begins from a state of stillness, for all activity begins in stillness, and what arises is an idea, a creative impulse. The composer reflects on this idea in the mind and through imagination enlarges and formalizes it according to the laws of music. At this point, according to Mozart, it is even possible to hear the entire piece as a whole. Then, taking into account the capabilities of each musical instrument and using the conventions of musical language, the composer gives the idea a form as musical notes written on paper.

A musician reads these notes. They are interpreted in the mind as music and, if the mind remains focused, the composer's complete vision can be appreciated. Then the musician, using his knowledge and skill in playing a musical instrument, transforms the notes written on the paper into sounds.

The final stage of the creative process involves the listener. He or she hears the physical sounds and recognizes the musical patterns. If the listening is fine, the music will have its intended emotional effect and the piece can be appreciated in full, as the composer intended. The satisfaction experienced by the listener brings a cycle of the creative process, which began as an idea in the composer's mind, to its natural conclusion.

Creativity in business

In the business context there are the same three steps. A creative idea begins in the mind of a designer and is then transformed by the production team into a product or service that satisfies a customer's need. This process can bring about the same satisfaction and fulfilment for the customer as is experienced by the listener to the music.

This creative process requires the application of intelligence and skills at each step of the way. This intelligence manifests differently depending on the nature of the creation.

In business the nature of the need is the determining factor. For an architect, the need is to create a design for a building that fulfils the requirements of practical usage, beauty and affordability. For the producer of a technology-based product like a mobile phone, the needs to be satisfied include functionality, technical feasibility, price and even fashion, the 'look and feel'. To be creative in business the solution must satisfy a need in a manner that is relevant, effective and appropriate for the time, place and budget of the customer. These are very practical rather than artistic considerations, yet to be creative in business requires the businessman or woman to apply consciousness in the moment in the same way as the poet or musician.

A further dimension to creativity in business is that a business by its nature is a co-operative effort. The good news is that the opportunities for creative action abound, not only for those in customer-facing roles but for all the supporting cast as well. The principles outlined apply on an individual basis and it is then the responsibility and function of management to co-ordinate the individual centres of creativity so that the sum of the parts becomes a unified whole. Communications thus play an important part in this integration process.

If there is not effective communication and close co-ordination between the various functions of a business organization, then a great deal of creative energy can be wasted. Without such communication, brilliantly designed products and services can languish 'on the shelf' because of uninspired sales and marketing or because the designers and engineers produced a very fine product, but without any reference to the real needs of the market.

Beauty, ingenuity, originality, intelligence and love are indicators of creativity and when they are manifest the result is unique. If something is produced that comes from habitual thinking, it will be a form of creation but it will not generate the same impact or benefit as will an action powered by conscious attention.

Chris had this experience:

> My company had worked for the Financial Services Authority in the late 1990s. We also had a lot of experience of helping our large clients manage their Year 2000 programmes. So, after reading in the press that the FSA was planning to try to ensure that regulated firms would be ready for the big day, we approached the FSA to offer them assistance with their regulatory functions. The person we met had just been appointed to the role and had not yet thought through how he was going to do his job. He asked us what we could do for him. This is a difficult, very open

question for a consultant, who is more used to answering the question, 'Can you do this piece of work?' My colleague and I asked the client some questions to discover as much as we could about his requirements and then undertook to respond in a few days.

When we returned to our office, we 'stood back' to consider his real needs, for we had no better idea of the answer to his question than he did. What then became clear was that it was pointless to offer to do his job for him. That had been our original idea, but we were not familiar with the workings of the regulated firms and did not have the resources to inspect every firm anyway. What we needed to do was to enable him to put the FSA inspectors in a position to do the job, as part of their normal inspection routine. So we proposed to him that we lay on a course for the inspectors. This would explain the real nature of the Y2K problem, remove the myth and the fear from which they were suffering as they were not IT specialists, and give them some simple tools with which to examine the programme plans and the performance of their firms in preparing for the millennium. This creative solution was accepted and proved very successful. We trained over 350 inspectors and almost all found it very helpful to them in their jobs.

The creation of wealth

We have defined the important role of business in a society as the creation of wealth for the benefit of all. We have presented a view of the creative process in the development of a product, service or a company. To round the circle out we are now going to present how a company might best contribute to the conscious creation of wealth for the benefit of all. The approach is summarised as a six-stage process.

The ideal situation in this action is that an actor, anyone in a business, is working in the present moment with concentrated attention and not from the past according to a fixed set of preconceived ideas. In this state the real need is seen without prejudices or preferences that confuse the process. The connection is made possible by the application of resources, both internal and external. If the full creative powers of the individual and the organization are free to operate, then resources can be effectively applied in meeting the need. The result will be satisfaction and happiness for supplier and the customer. If any of these powers are missing then the result will be partial and if they are mainly absent then the result could have negative consequences. Boldness is needed to strike out on a new way, free from mechanical repetition. Such an action will be fresh and ever new. This is true creativity.

We set out below the steps in this process. You will note a distinct similarity in this process described from the perspective of creativity with the previous examples given in the road map from Principles to Profit, and the discussion of the complete cycle of service. The same principles are in play; all that changes is the vantage point.

The steps to creating wealth for all

1. IDENTIFY THE NEED

It all begins with the need. The need must be seen clearly, objectively and in some depth. This is facilitated by a deeper perception of the nature of the prospective customer and discrimination between what is wanted and what is genuinely needed. Service to a customer begins from the initial contact by listening carefully and asking penetrating questions that help them to recognize the true nature of their need.

2. APPLY CONSCIOUS EFFORT

The creative process is the application of natural resources, including human intelligence, in the development of a solution for the need. The perception of the need, the assessment of the resources available and the development and implementation of the solution are all powered by one essential energy, often called consciousness, that is available to everyone. It is best accessed when the mind is still, poised and alert.

3. WORK FROM PRINCIPLE

In a business the implementation of a creative solution usually requires a team effort, with groups of people working together towards a common aim. If the members of the group share common values and work from these principles, if they are also competent in their respective areas and if there exists a high degree of mutual trust, then it is more likely that the solution will be creative and therefore relevant, effective and beneficial for the customer.

4. ACT WITH INTEGRITY IN THE MOMENT

To produce the finest result all members of the team need to act with full integrity, that is, honestly and ethically, assuming full responsibility for their actions and executing them with full attention: acting consciously in the present moment.

5. TEAMWORK – GIVE PRAISE GENEROUSLY

Working as a cohesive team means that the individual claims such as my performance, my results are dropped in favour of concern for the whole – the cumulative efforts of the group, be it the department, region or company. Praise can be a powerful stimulant to creativity if it is given generously and received in such a way as not to give support to the individual ego. Just observe the impact on people when they are rightfully praised. They grow in stature and confidence before your very eyes.

> From praise comes joy, from joy – strength, from strength –
> virtue, from virtue – purity and from purity comes realiza-
> tion of one's full potential.
>
> Leon MacLaren, *The Machinery of Government*, 1998

Given the mutual respect and love that grows when people work this way in a group, the power of the group grows and is available for each member to draw upon.

6. WORK IN THE SERVICE OF ALL

Keeping in mind that service is for all is vital. One of the best ways to reinforce this point is to acknowledge our duty of care for all the stakeholders in our business: the employees, suppliers, customers, the community (including the environment) as well as the shareholders. This leads to the realization that your customers are also duty bound to act in such a way as to benefit their stakeholders. This memory of service to everyone will help direct the creative process towards a solution that is of mutual benefit, and which satisfies the need for service to the fullest.

Happy at work

Many have heard of E.F Schumacher's seminal work, *Small is Beautiful* but not all have read another of his perceptive works, *Good Work* (1979). In that book he presents three purposes of work:

- To provide necessary and useful goods and services
- To perfect our gifts, i.e. develop our talents
- To serve, in co-operation with others

This direction to use our gifts in the service of others was given in the Bible:

> Whichever gift each of you has received, use it in the service of one another, like good stewards dispensing the grace of God in its various forms.
>
> St Paul, Epistle to Peter

People are most creative when they are doing the work that suits them best, the work that best expresses their talents. You therefore need to ask yourself and each member of the team whether you are enjoying your work. Are you engaged in a way that makes best use of your talents?

We all have special talents but for many they are waiting to be discovered. We cannot choose our talents, but we can choose either to recognize them or to ignore them. Talents cannot be learned in the same way as skills, but they can be developed so that their full potential is realized. For a few this is obvious, for many, less so. To go through life without ever knowing or expressing our talent is evidently a waste.

> Everyone has been made for some particular work and the
> desire for that work resides in the heart.
>
> Jalaluddin Rumi in Whinfield, 1975

Here is an exercise that may help you in that direction, whatever stage in our career you have reached.

Read the following questions carefully, one at a time, quietly considering the answers that arise in the mind. Write down your answers. Allow sufficient time between one question and the next so that you can give full attention to each question.

- What do you respond to with energy and enthusiasm?
- What moves you?
- What inspirations and intuitions most enliven you?
- What seems most natural to you?
- What is effortless, comes spontaneously and produces natural joy?

It is important to consider these things. These questions and what follows will form the basis for further self-examination.

Your vocation or calling does not necessarily have to be your 'day job', but to live an harmonious and fulfilling life, your work should at least not be in conflict with your talents and innermost longings. Of course, the ideal is that we should love our work.

> Your task in life is to discover your work and then with all
> your heart to give yourself to it.
>
> The Buddha, cit. in Boldt, 1993

To discover and learn more about the work you love, you must carefully observe and attend to life in the moment. It is all too easy to fall into a mechanical way of responding to life based on an accumulation of past experiences or future imaginings.

There are many examples of children being deflected from their real vocation by comments, criticisms or advice from well-meaning family, teachers or friends. These early impressions can cover the true talents, the way clouds hide the ever-shining sun.

A common blight on creativity and happiness in work is working for the wrong motive such as working only for the money. While this may be a necessity for some, for others, where it is not necessary, it becomes a real burden.

How can you tell if your work is right for you? How can you make your work an expression of your deepest Self?

> You will know if you have found your calling – if you are
> happy. Profound joy of heart is like a magnet that indicates
> the path of life. One has to follow it even though one enters
> into a way full of difficulties.
>
> Mother Teresa, cit. in Boldt, 1993

To be creative is natural for us all. While it is natural to create, we all too often nullify the process by our interference, usually in the form of fixed ideas about the task or person before us. To be creative requires a trust in our true nature and a willingness to act without fear.

> Whatever you can do, or dream you can, begin it. Boldness
> has genius, power and magic in it. Begin it now.
>
> attributed to Johann Wolfgang von Goethe

If you can act in this way, fearlessly and boldly in the present, you will be truly free to express yourself. Being true to yourself is the highest and best service you can offer to others. This full self-expression is naturally joyous and when you are doing something you love, you want it to be the best possible offering and you are willing to make whatever effort is necessary. Being thus contented and fulfilled, one naturally turns outward and the motivation becomes focused on extending to others – a natural generosity.

Creativity can come from surprising sources, as a friend of ours relates:

'Ten years ago I left the corporate world to travel and write. However it seems that travelling and writing won't pay my bills. I've been very fortunate, finding work whenever I've needed it. Although corporate work is not my passion, I've always secretly enjoyed it. Some of my recent work for a drinks company – innovative holographic gift packs – won praise from the chief executive as 'fantastic' and 'stunning'.

'How could this be? How could a part-time, occasional, temporary freelancer cause such a stir? To be honest, I didn't do anything really special. I gave attention to detail, focusing on one thing at a time, being persistent. But I had also, more than ever, gone beyond my own opinions and actively gauged those of many others. Everyone has something to add, especially those traditionally left out. I didn't do it for show, or to be politically correct. I did it to obtain their input, and out of a genuine wish to include them, in a way that wasn't always the case for me when I was younger: I was myopic, weedy, balding, uncool, useless at sport.

'I had of course shown the concepts, designs, colours and finishes for these new packs to our main international customers. But in addition to this, I had shown the packs to everyone else too, and remained open to their thoughts. I took a very personal approach – walking around, showing people, asking their opinions. I talked to everyone, to my boss, my subordinate, our PA, the designers, the printers, the office manager, the receptionist, the postman and the chef.

'The result of all this was plenty of goodwill towards myself, my brand, my new packs – and our pensive chief executive impressed as well. The word from the retail street is that these are by far the best new drinks packs on shelf this year, sparkling out at consumers from 20 metres. Though corporate work is not my passion it can indeed be rewarding and exciting. The root of the word religion is the Latin *religare*, meaning to bind or connect. In the creation of these new packs I have, I believe, in my own way, behaved religiously.'

Summary

We have attempted to show that creativity arises naturally when people are working in a positive and supportive environment that has service as its focus. This environment is established when the organisation's stated principles and values are of the order discussed in the previous chapters, agreed by all and used as the basis for the day to day decisions in the life of the company. People working in this way have the best opportunity to discover and develop their innate talents. When this happens they are most likely to be happy, enthusiastic and efficient in the execution of their duties and to help others achieve their aims as well.

The next step is to look at the role of the moral manager, the different aspects of the role and the principles which should guide his or her actions. This is the subject of Chapter Eleven.

CHAPTER 11 - THE MORAL MANAGER:

We have examined the challenges facing us as individuals engaged in business. We have also looked at those problems experienced by companies attempting to create wealth ethically but profitably, and touched upon the difficulties that exist in a society as a whole when trust in business is eroded.

In attempting to discover ways in which to respond to these challenges, we have sought guidance from a variety of sources, secular and spiritual, concerning the key principles that should be governing our thoughts, speech and action and for practical guidance in helping to bring better balance to business activities. A common concern is the question of how a business can operate with integrity while still exercising its duty of care to all stakeholders. This care is expressed by providing an excellent service for customers, a good return to investors and a creative, stable environment for staff to work and grow.

The spirit of a group, be it a department, a business unit or a company, reflects the spirit of its leadership. Just as a work of art reveals the consciousness that went into its creation and the spirit of the artist, so it is with a business. The competence and quality of the management team determines to a great extent the performance and sustainability of an organization. It is by no means the only factor, but it is probably the single most important one.

We shall now focus on the qualities and characteristics of a moral manager; someone who practises the art of moral management not only by managing resources and people, but also by leading and teaching.

LEADER, ORGANIZER, TEACHER

The key questions are:

- What are the functions of a manager?
- What are the guiding principles of a moral manager?
- How does a moral manager think, speak and act?

There have been many sources for the development of this approach. We have gained considerable insight from the teaching of great philosophers, particularly Plato, who wrote extensively on the nature, training and behaviour of the leaders of society, whom he called Guardians. In Plato's view it was necessary for the sake of society that leaders were virtuous so that they might set the proper example for everyone else. Virtue and goodness were natural to the human being, but ignorance of this caused men to become confused and agitated, leading to those actions that were the very opposite of virtuous.

> Is there a more suitable guideline for correct management than the interest of the community and everything that serves that interest?
>
> *Plato*, Republic

The functions of a manager

A manager performs a number of functions or roles which we group under three categories; as a leader, as an organizer and as a teacher. For the very senior executives in large, publicly-listed companies there will naturally be more of a requirement for leadership and for teaching. For the managing director of a small, private company, all the roles may be played by one person. A middle manager may need to place more emphasis on organizing. But all three are present in every managerial assignment; it is just the mix and emphasis that differs.

- The **manager as leader**: the current emphasis in business schools is on leadership development, which has replaced management training as the focus of executive development programmes. Managers lead by providing the vision, establishing the direction and the goals, setting out the route and providing the necessary resources to enable the group to realize its goals. The leader establishes the principles, the plans and policies to enable the vision to be realized.

- The **manager as organizer**: included here is the responsibility for the organization and application of the resources necessary to execute the plan. The organizer is not just concerned with efficiency. The function includes both operational command and control as well as effective people management; it includes the use of the head and the heart; it concerns quality as well as quantity; it requires that the agreed principles are lived in practice.

- The **manager as teacher**: this involves the important responsibility of facilitating the growth and development of the staff for whom the manager is responsible. This work benefits both the company and the individual. When knowledge and skills are passed on, not only is productivity improved but the next generation of leaders is developed. As with any teacher, the manager must learn as well as teach, listen as well as speak. In this way the manager's knowledge and skills improve too.

The guiding principles of a moral manager

What should be the basic principles that form the basis for the performance of any of these functions? Here we return to our four fundamental virtues which are at the heart of all spiritual traditions, now expressed in the context of moral management.

TRUTH

Speak the truth, be totally honest with yourself and others inside and outside the company and maintain your personal integrity and that of the company in all situations.

> The first quality of a leader of people – always the first quality – is a devotion to truth.
>
> Leon MacLaren, 1978a

LOVE

Show care, service and goodwill to all, which includes employees, suppliers, customers, business colleagues, members of the community, society and nation and, importantly, your family.

> Remember that your servants are men, equal to you in origin and that the human species, which is by nature free, ought not to be, indeed cannot be, united by any fear, but only by love.
>
> Marsilio Ficino, writing to the young Cardinal Riario (Ficino, Vol. 4)

JUSTICE

Never do to others what you would not have them do to you. Serve to be served, respect to be respected, obey to be obeyed.

> Great leaders are first and foremost servants and this is the key to their greatness.
>
> Robert Greenleaf, *The Servant as Leader*, 1970

FREEDOM

Act in such a way as to be free from fear, pride, selfishness, arrogance, dependence on the opinion of others, weakness and negative criticism. Referring to these negative qualities, Sun Tzu wrote in his *Art of War*:

> Nourish your soldiers and build up their internal strength so
> that they are free of hundreds of diseases and this will ensure
> victory.
>
> Sun Tzu, cit. in Kheng-Hor, 1997

How should a moral manager think, speak and act?

The distinguishing mark of a moral manager is that as you think so you speak, and as you speak so you act. To put that into effect, these general principles will help:

1. Work from principle in all endeavours. This means not only the principles underlying the company values but also those commonly held principles of the society in which you are operating. If you are working in a global market this means that you need to learn about the values of other societies with which you deal.

2. Act virtuously. To do so is not only consistent with your nature, that is to say, most natural, but also the most efficient means of action. Setting an example for others to follow is more effective than all the mission statements and social responsibility policies that anyone could devise.

3. Use a balanced approach: balance the apparently opposite qualities of rational and emotional; knowledge and being, discipline and love. This is further developed below.

4. Create a work environment that is conducive to selfless service, creativity, quality and value, trust, self-development, learning and teaching, social responsibility, harmony.

5. Be courageous – take well-calculated risks when necessary and be indifferent to any praise or blame based on the results.

6. Act in ways that are rooted in consideration for the welfare of others.

7. Look to your responsibilities rather than your privileges, to your duties rather than your rights.

8. Learn and teach. Be open to learn from all and be ready to give freely of your knowledge to all.

9. Be yourself.

In essence the message is that to be a moral manager, you need to work from fine principles and values for the common good.

Getting the balance right

In management publications today, the concept of 'emotional intelligence', the caring side of management, has become very popular. In recent years there has been a swing away from the rational, logical, systematic approach to management in favour of the feeling and emotional aspects. We were certainly in need of such an impulse and as long as the pendulum does not swing too far in that direction, this initiative will produce a more rounded perspective. The risk is that it will swing too far the other way, reason will be lost and the balance with it.

In our view, what is most important in bringing about positive change is to strike the right balance between apparently opposite qualities. There needs to be a dynamic balance between the rational and the emotional aspects of business, just as we need to establish a similar balance within each of us. This is the real challenge for the moral manager.

Throwing a pot on a potter's wheel is a good model of balanced application which can be applied by analogy to love and discipline. The inner hand is love which naturally brings about expansion. The outer hand is the discipline which helps bring about the appropriate form. If there is too much love, i.e. too much pressure from the inner hand, then the resultant pot will be formless and may be so weakened that it cannot fulfil its purpose as a pot. In the same way if there is too much discipline from the outer hand, the result will be small, lacking beauty and wrongly shaped for its function. The need is for a dynamic balance.

Here are just some of the delicate issues that need balancing at both the individual and company level:

Command/control	vs	Caring/compassion
Doing	vs	Delegating/empowering
Financial performance	vs	Social responsibility
Logical thinking	vs	Intuitive response
Risk averse	vs	Innovative
Tradition	vs	Change
Teaching	vs	Learning
Maintaining	vs	Creating new
Discipline	vs	Love
Trusting in technology	vs	Trusting in people

A profile of the moral manager

We shall now try to draw together our profile of the ideal moral manager in terms of specific qualities and behaviours. This is the detailed response to the questions about the way you should think, speak and act. The diagram below shows how the four universal principles manifest themselves as twelve virtues, which in turn flower as thirty-six fine qualities of our moral manager. These qualities, which also describe behaviours, show that half are more related to the head and the other half to the heart.

While it is unlikely that any of us will possess all these qualities to their full measure, we all have some of both kinds. By being aware of the full complement, and understanding how their application epitomizes the moral manager, we may each be motivated to improve our state across the board.

Four universal principles

Those relating to the head:

Truth   **Justice**

Those relating to the heart:

Love   **Freedom**

These four universal principles then manifest themselves as twelve virtues:

TRUTH
- Honest
- Temperate
- Reasonable

JUSTICE
- Patient
- Respectful
- Responsible

LOVE
- Magnanimous
- Compassionate
- Tolerant

FREEDOM
- Loyal
- Creative
- Courageous

Eighteen qualities relating to truth and justice (the head)

The six qualities relating to truth and justice manifest themselves as behaviours, i.e. as thoughts, words and deeds:

TRUTH	**HONEST**	Transparent Accountable Trustworthy
	TEMPERATE	Self-controlled Discriminating Disciplined
	REASONABLE	Intelligent Fair-minded Obedient
JUSTICE	**PATIENT**	Steadfast Persistent Forgiving
	RESPECTFUL	Honourable Perceptive Courteous
	RESPONSIBLE	Confident Dutiful Mature

Eighteen qualities relating to love and freedom (the heart)

The six qualities relating to love and freedom manifest themselves as behaviours of a more emotional nature:

LOVE

MAGNANIMOUS
- Benevolent
- Friendly
- Open-hearted

COMPASSIONATE
- Receptive
- Supportive
- Caring

TOLERANT
- Gentle
- Calm
- Humble

FREEDOM

LOYAL
- Conscientious
- Sincere
- Faithful

CREATIVE
- Imaginative
- Adaptive
- Innovative

COURAGEOUS
- Determined
- Enthusiastic
- Committed

We can sum up these relationships in the following diagram:

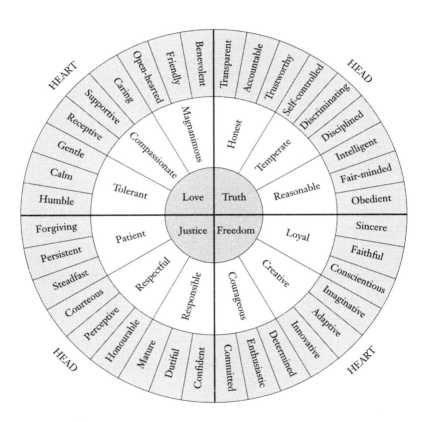

If virtue is natural, why do we not see more of it?

What we are proposing is that these qualities arise naturally when we are involved in any endeavour. It is true that experience would indicate that they are not often manifested. In fact their opposites are more likely to be called 'normal behaviour' due to their continual presence. It seems that we make mistakes when we choose something other than these qualities. This means that we mistake one thing for another, we literally mis-take it.

These are some of our more important mistakes that help explain why the goodness inherent in these qualities is not so obvious.

WE MISTAKE INFORMATION FOR KNOWLEDGE

Knowledge is used here in the sense of real understanding which arises in practice. For example, there was once a group of philosophers who decided to learn to play tennis. They read all about the game and studied pictures and diagrams showing how the various strokes were played. They then proceeded to the tennis court and began to play. Not surprisingly, they found that they had no control over the ball which, when they did manage to hit it, either went into the net or out of court. After a short time they concluded that the game of tennis was a foolish one and thoroughly unsatisfactory. They had the information about how to play but not the knowledge, which can only be acquired by putting the information into practice.

WE MISTAKE CONTINUAL ACTIVITY FOR FULLNESS OF LIFE

It is natural and good for life to be full. A life which is empty is unsatisfying and lonely. But what does this fullness consist of? For example a life with love, peace, wisdom, value to others and light could properly be called full. A common mistake is to take activity for fullness and the result is busy-ness. People fill up their lives with one activity after another without any rest between them. It is not that activity is bad in itself, but the undue value and importance given to it is the mistake. Activity for activity's sake can be just senseless.

Another view was expressed by Lao Tse who said:

> The way of the wise is to work by being still.
>
> Lao Tse, *The Sayings of Lao Tse*, 1972 edn.

WE MISTAKE SERVITUDE FOR SERVICE.

Service is natural and everyone loves to be of service. There is no real contentment in selfishness. However, service is often thought of as being the same as servitude, one step away from being a slave. The result is that people shy away from service instead of accepting it as a natural part of life.

> Man finds happiness only in serving his neighbour. And he
> finds it there because rendering service to his neighbours, he
> is in communion with the divine spirit that lives in them.
>
> Leo Tolstoy, cit in *The Eternal Wisdom*

WE MISTAKE AN ATTITUDE OF 'GIVING TO GET' FOR GENEROSITY

Real generosity is giving without any hope or expectation of anything in return. It is not just being generous with money, time or anything else, but generosity of spirit that is important. This means being open and available to everyone, seeing the best in people and responding to that. It involves giving attention, time and love to others without any ulterior motive. Where there is the idea of giving in order to get something in return, this true generosity of spirit is covered up and with it, the person's true nature.

> We make a living by what we get, but we make a life by what we give.
>
> Winston Churchill, *Their Finest Hour*, 2002 edn.

WE MISTAKE NOT CARING FOR DETACHMENT

Detachment is often confused with not caring. But detachment in its true sense is the key to caring. For example, a doctor may be a highly trained and disciplined person, working selflessly for his patients. If a patient is cured he does not seek a certificate of success to show his greatness as a doctor. Equally, if a patient dies he will be sorry but will not give way to excessive grief or lamentation. Were he to do so, his ability to care for other patients would be impaired. In the same way, if we become bound up or identified with our desires or feelings, it can actually reduce our capacity to care for others. It also easily leads to misery when those desires or feelings are frustrated or when they contradict each other.

WE MISTAKE MONEY FOR WEALTH

Money is a part of wealth, but by no means its entirety. Wealth also includes such things as an abundance of love, wisdom, goodwill and generosity of spirit. A man or woman with a great deal of money who is hard-hearted and mean cannot truly be called wealthy. Nor is such a person happy. In fact if you have enough money, you are wealthy. If you do not have enough, however much money you have, you are poor.

WE MISTAKE THE OPINION OF OTHERS FOR SELF-RESPECT

It is perfectly good and natural to have self-respect. This means that one is thinking, speaking and acting in a way that is being true to oneself. When a person has self-respect, the opinion of others does not matter. On the other hand, living in the opinion of others is a kind of tyranny. One is forever fearful of what they will think. A tremendous effort is made to impress them. The slightest remark or comment, which may have been quite unintentional, can have devastating consequences on one's confidence.

There is a poem by Mother Teresa that illustrates this:

People are often unreasonable, illogical and self-centred;

Forgive them anyway.

If you are kind, people may accuse you of selfish, ulterior motives;

Be kind anyway.

If you are successful, you will win some false friends and some true enemies;

Succeed anyway.

If you are honest and frank, people may cheat you;

Be honest and frank anyway.

What you spend years building, someone may destroy overnight;

Build anyway.

If you find serenity and happiness, they may be jealous;

Be happy anyway.

The good you do today, people will often forget tomorrow;

Do good anyway.

Give the world the best you have, and it may never be enough;

Give the world the best you've got anyway.

You see, in the final analysis, it is all between you and God;

It was never between you and them anyway.

Mother Teresa, *In the Final Analysis*

WE MISTAKE SPEED FOR EFFICIENCY

Efficiency does not necessarily mean just getting everything done quickly. Sometimes it is necessary to make careful preparations so that the action will be effective and have the desired result. Doing things too fast often leads to poor results in the long term. It usually turns out to be ineffective and the action has to begin again. This often involves sorting out the mess caused by the hasty action.

WE MISTAKE WORK AS A MEANS OF SURVIVAL FOR WORK AS A MEANS OF FULFILMENT

When people love their work it is a means of fulfilment and satisfaction. Being fully, usefully and purposefully engaged results in happiness and contentment. If the idea is that work is essentially drudgery and that it is only done because it is necessary for survival, then this natural contentment is lost. Work then does become drudgery. It is not fulfilling.

To list the issues and the mistakes is the easy part. The question is, 'How can you make the right choice more often?'

Making the right choice

We have some ideas for your consideration that have been offered to us through our philosophy studies, which we have tested in our own lives and have recently shared with the participants in our Philosophy in Business courses.

The essence of the advice is to be in the present moment. If that sounds easy then you will need to begin observing your decision-making process. What we believe you will find is that for a good deal of the time the mind is either dwelling on past experiences or imagining what will happen in the future.

You may notice that when you make a decision, your mind and emotional set-up tend to call upon selective aspects of your past experience. These may be based on pre-conceived ideas or feelings about a person or a situation. While these old ideas and feelings dominate, you are unable to take an objective view of the actual conditions that are facing you at this time and in this place. This is what you might call 'thinking and being in the box'.

What we recommend is bringing the mind to rest, without the memories and imaginings, and looking with full attention at what is facing you. In our experience the stillness which results creates space in the mind and enables the emotions to stabilize. This gives greater clarity and penetration. Like Mozart, our best ideas and perceptions come to us when we are at ease.

Begin to discover this for yourself through the simple practice of connecting with one of your senses in the moment; listening to the sounds entering the ears, feeling the touch of the finger on the mouse button, seeing the words on a page, in the present. Allow the sensations to arise without any judgements or interpretations. As you practise this you will observe how the mind habitually moves about and is rarely fully present and connected. You may also become aware of the constant commenting that goes on, like a background noise. This commentary can easily distract you from the present consideration.

When you are able to withdraw your attention from the distractions and concentrate in the present, it will be possible to reflect on the issue at hand. This does not mean reeling off a huge list of comparative thoughts about the subject; it has to do with looking at the issues with a quiet mind. It is in this state that the mind is able to operate at its highest level.

This approach is used in martial arts training. The combatant is taught to remain centred and not anticipate the direction or nature of the opponent's attack, but rather to be in a full state of readiness, so that when the attack comes, all one's attention is available to respond. This does not mean that one's experience will not be brought to bear if it is relevant. Operating in the moment with full attention on the specific issue you will become conscious of what particular aspects of your experience are needed. Indeed relevant experiences will be there automatically, called up by the need in front of you. Please refer back to the story of Matajuro on page 35 to see how he was trained to become the greatest swordsman in the land.

Our experience shows that the power of habit is very great. It is not an easy process to make decisions in the present moment, free from mechanical thinking and emotional baggage. But through practice you can gradually develop a finer sense of discrimination between right and wrong; good and bad; natural and normal.

We use only a small part of our intellectual and emotional power. In our experience it is the dissipation of fine energies through lack of attention that is the cause. What we are seeking through these simple exercises is a greater ability to marshal, in a balanced way, our rational and emotional forces. The finer discrimination thus attained will not only help us to make better business decisions but also bring light in all other aspects of our lives.

CHAPTER 12 - FROM PRINCIPLES

Throughout the book we have given examples from our own experience, as well as those of a number of our business friends and colleagues. In this chapter we present some further examples of the latter.

Several wrote about the central importance of *truth* and *honesty* in their lives, their experiences of being pressured to depart from the truth and their acute discomfort in such situations. In several cases they left well-paid positions rather than do what they knew was wrong.

There is no such thing as a little lie

'I had the opportunity to buy a smaller competitor, which was in a fast-growing section of the market and had a lot of potential. When I was looking at their books as part of the due diligence, I noticed some padding, minor things but they were not completely honest. It caused me to wonder what else they knew that they were not telling me and I walked away from the deal. That company went on to become much bigger than mine, very successful, very well known . . . and then imploded in a sea of red ink and corruption.'

Honesty is the best policy

'I worked for a large computer manufacturer. I had to tell my boss that we could not do what a customer wanted, for internal reasons. What should we tell them? He said "tell them

TO PROFIT IN PRACTICE

the truth." Lying is far too complicated because either you have to cover up (and remember what you are covering up) or you get caught out, and will not be trusted in future.'

Reflections on truth and honesty

'Very early in my life I connected with integrity. My father was a man of high integrity and his example in our home and surrounding social interaction grounded me for my life. Truth and honesty were values I took to heart. Years later in my study of philosophy and theology I came to appreciate how lucky I was to have that early influence, for the great traditions espouse the importance of such virtues. This strengthened my resolve to be faithful to what I knew was important to my purpose for living.

'I was a partner in an accounting firm. In the initial years of being admitted to the partnership, besides the challenge of funding my capital, I was faced with a challenge of a different sort. I learned that a "tax planning mechanism" was available to those in the partnership wishing to reduce their tax bill. It was based on establishing a trust to divert some of the income stream to a lower area of taxation. Many partners were involved. Certain tax partners had given it the OK but it didn't sit well with me. My enquiry through discussion with my tax partners and my own reading of the law had led me to question its morality.

'I remember the deliberation process – there were monetary gains, many partners were availing themselves of the option, the tax partners had spotted a so-called gap in the tax laws that appeared legitimate. It was tempting. But I just couldn't do it. The feeling in the pit of my stomach was terrible as I contemplated the opportunity. Thank God I decided against it. I could have carried that feeling, that burden with me for the ensuing years of my professional life, reinforced each year at tax return time. No doubt the benefit in monetary terms was substantial. However I never regretted my decision not to partake. I would not have been able to live with myself. I would have been "crossing the line" in what I valued.

'Later, the partnership was going through one of its down cycles. Business generally was tough and the accounting business was feeling the pinch. The managing partner at the time was setting about his task – close control of costs (tighten spending, cut the dead wood, chop off a few heads), get income up (get the whips out and get those billable hours up!). So it came about there was a tremendous focus on billable hours. To add to the pressure, partners' productivity percentages were produced weekly and were circulated to every partner for scrutiny and to see for themselves "who's not performing". The effect was peer pressure and competition to get productivity up. This focus was not only at partner level: all levels of staff were being heavily monitored and therefore pressured.

'This of course brought temptation to "fudge a little" on

your daily time sheet. If hours were a little low at the end of the day, a half-hour here to this client, a half-hour there to that client would easily do the trick. This sounds shocking and perhaps it was done in more subtle ways, but the result was that clients could be billed for work hours that were not fully given.

'Everyone felt the pressure. With my productivity figures lower than those of many of my peers, I felt pressure. Having worked in close proximity to many partners whose work hours were not greater than mine, I couldn't help but wonder how their productivity levels could be much different. There had to be fudging.

'Once again I couldn't do it. I just couldn't live with what was virtually cheating – padding one's billable time. Eventually I confronted the powers that be and stated my position. I would only charge time to a client code if I actually felt that I had given a full unit's worth of work and my staff were instructed to do likewise.

'As I reflect back on that down period I cannot help but think that I couldn't have been the only one that knew that being "more liberal" with billable hours was wrong. I query this, not to pass judgment on my fellow partners but to have compassion for those partners and staff who carried the burden of knowing that what they did was wrong. Mind you, there was no directive as such to cheat and the firm was one that aspired to high professional standards. Nevertheless I have no doubt that many succumbed to increasing productivity in this way. When I think of it, the partnership was not a happy ship in those times and perhaps this burden contributed to the general unhappiness.

'In the longer term of course things moved on and the partnership came to understand, if not the moral aspect, at least that you don't bite the hand that feeds you. If you push too hard on inflated fees you lose clients. They also recognized that the management of unbillable time is more productive than trying to force billable time because that's where the avenues for growth lie.

'As I ponder over what I have written, what comes to me is a recollection of what Pope John Paul II stated in one of his encyclicals:

> The relationship between man's freedom and God's law is most deeply lived out in the 'heart' of the person, in his moral conscience. As the Second Vatican Council observed: 'In the depths of his conscience man detects a law which he does not impose on himself, but which holds him to obedience. Always summoning him to love good and avoid evil, the voice of conscience can when necessary speak to his heart more specifically: 'do this, shun that'. For man has in his heart a law written by God. To obey it is the very dignity of man; according to it he will be judged (cf. Rom 2:14–16).
>
> Pope John Paul II, *Veritatis Splendor*

Morality is founded on faith

'I have always striven for honesty in all things. When I discovered the teachings of Torah [the law given to Moses] late in life, I realized with a shock that morality is the basis of Judaism and indeed of civilization. It is fundamental to business.

'I had grown up without religion and confused. My father was a completely non-religious Jew, a socialist in South Africa. But he was the most moral man I ever knew. He was moral to a fault and would do things that were not in his interest, if they were the right thing to do. Then about twelve years ago, I would be working at my desk with a classical music station on the radio in the background. On Friday evenings there was a Jewish Sabbath service. Gradually I came to listen to it in the foreground and it aroused my interest in Judaism. Now I am active and observant. And now I recognize that my father's morality, which I imbibed without realizing it, all came from his Judaism, though he never admitted it.'

Others commented on the importance of trust in business.

Trust in a new media creative agency

'In the creative fields, where innovation differentiates, trust and reputation are critical. Clients are often commissioning work that they have no experience with. They come to the agency with a request to create something 'new'. They can't describe what they want but can only describe their need or problem. This is not dissimilar to a patient/doctor relationship. Patients can only describe how they feel. They don't know what their ailment is. Only the doctor can analyse what it is and how to cure it.

'So what builds trust and reputation in business?

'When a business truly acts in the best interests of its clients, its recommendations are focused on what will benefit the client, not themselves. Profit is the result, not the cause, of good work. This does not mean agreeing to unprofitable work. But it does mean advising the client not to proceed with projects that are not worth the expenditure or will not bring the required results. Our experience in turning down ill-conceived projects is that the client does return. And when they return with a subsequent project, it is with a clearer brief that we can develop effectively. This honesty builds relationships. The client realizes that you are acting in their best interests. They relax and rely on your guidance and judgement. Reputation is built in small steps.

'When a business truly acts in the best interests of its staff, this builds strong teams and loyalty. When your people speak in the "we/our" voice there is a commitment that is reflected in both their work and their attitudes. Our business operates with a transparent balance sheet. Our people know when we are making a profit and when we are not. In prosperous times, expenses are allowed that are not even requested when they know that money is tight. The directors are the first to cut costs by example and postpone their salaries to improve cash flow. Because the directors are willing to make sacrifices to keep the business operating, the employees are committed to success and steadfast in lean times. This opens flexible ways of working and remuneration schemes that support life choices. The human factor and the bottom line are viewed in tandem when cut-backs are required.

'When a business truly acts in the best interest of the community, its contributions are part of the company persona and the staff's sense of purpose. We endeavour to do one project a year at cost for a business or charity that would not be able to afford our services. The criteria for selection are that the project must:

● use our new media skills to bring a project into the community that will have a positive effect;

● be satisfying to the staff producing it, either because of its purpose or the creative opportunity, or both;

● be an example of fine work to raise the standard and show what is possible in our field.

'To date, this endeavour has produced work of a very high standard that has benefited our clients, our people and the community at large.

'Business is a complex environment fraught with challenges. In some ways it is mechanical, led by ideas that can be very small minded. But it is also an open playing field in which those running the businesses have the opportunity to create new models for working, models that can have a strong impact in demonstrating how true principles can be the basis for company policies, visions and standards. Managing by example is known to be the most direct way to influence thinking and bring about change. So those of us in a position to take the lead in creating work relationships based on these true principles are most fortunate.'

We have noted that the customs in other cultures are often different from ours, but that the *essential values* are the same. This is borne out by this experience.

Family loyalty does not mean nepotism

'When acting as consultant to the Ministry of Planning in a Middle-Eastern country, we were calling for tenders for the refurbishment of their head office interiors. In discussing the tender list with the minister he asked me to include his cousin on the tender list. This seemed to be a process of nepotism, and I expressed concern. The minister pointed out that in their culture support for one's family was a prime ethical requirement. I expressed concern that his cousin's organization was not capable of carrying out the contract. The problem was resolved when I suggested that I knew of a capable Spanish contractor, who was looking for a local partner. They formed a partnership, and tendered for the project. They were unsuccessful in their bid, but were satisfied that their duties to their relative had been satisfied, and made no attempt to negotiate a contract.'

The examples of adherence to the truth quoted above frequently required **courage**. But courage can be called upon in other situations too.

You can learn from every situation

'I was Vice President of Communications for an investment bank in New York. I was politically side-lined by a new colleague who had just joined the bank and was very envious of my position. Her intent was to humiliate, discredit and eventually fire me. I consulted a friend and guide who advised me to continue to go to work and face the situation since it clearly held within it a lesson I needed to learn. She said I could walk away from the bank once the lesson was learnt but not before. Under no circumstances, should I run away from this uncomfortable situation.

'I followed her instructions and kept going to work, facing all sorts of difficulties. But ever watchful, it definitely broke through some barriers that had to be dissolved on my part, like pride and over-attachment and identification with titles, privilege, etc. After three months, some very senior and influential friends at the bank were horrified at how I was being treated and arranged for me to be sent to London on an indefinite assignment. It ended up lasting a year during which time I found I loved London and found a position here. The new company paid for all moving expenses, bought me a flat and a car and gave me a start in the London market. A year later I started my own business.'

A spiritual company

Finally we will hear from a number of managers and consultants of a Dutch career counselling consultancy which attempts to live and work by the highest philosophical principles. In 2005 an International Spirit at Work award was presented to this company. These annual awards are co-sponsored by four organisations: The Association for Spirit at Work, The Spirit in Business Institute, The

World Business Academy and the European Baha'i Business Forum.

The criteria for the award are that the company must:

- have at least 60 full time employees and be at least five years old
- demonstrate both vertical and horizontal dimensions of Spirituality in the organisation
- have sustained the explicitly spiritual project, policy or practice being acknowledged for at least one year
- have a long term commitment to continuing Spirit at Work initiatives
- be considered exemplary in its commitment to Spirit at Work.

As part of the award application, letters from employees were required, setting out their experiences in working for the organisation. What follow are excerpts from some of these letters.

The comments of the employees seem to confirm that the conditions created in this organization are conducive to the spiritual, intellectual and emotional development of its staff and that this has resulted in the enhancement of their capabilities and confidence to provide a meaningful service to their clients. This is an example of a company working from Principles to Profit.

(The clients in these comments are the individuals being counselled. Many of the managers and consultants started as clients, people who had lost their jobs and were being counselled by the firm to help them to get back into work, and ended working for the firm.)

'Reflection: Before every office and work meetings we reflect on a relevant theme.

'This short meditation at the beginning of a meeting and

the subsequent sharing of each other's thoughts, visions and feelings provide us with an atmosphere of openness, a sense of safety where I feel I can say anything, even difficult and personal things. This extra dimension, beside all the professional discussion, makes our communication clearer and more effective.

'The questions about my feelings I experience as highly personal attention which helps me to develop my own thinking because I am invited to go more deeply. Very inspiring!

'In this company we live by shared values. They are the guidelines we use when questions arise and problems need to be solved. Because these shared values are based on the wisdom of world traditions they regularly prove themselves to be excellent guidelines. They help us to distance ourselves from the menial, from tediousness and to bring us to wise decisions. The shared values provide the direction to the way we fulfil our mission and our work.

'I have discovered that my place in the world is that of accompanying people rather than managing them. I still enjoy achieving results, but I have discovered that when I give attention, time and love to my clients and to the way I do my work, I am happier than when reaching a goal. More and more it is my inner compass which defines the direction I want to walk: to become a truly free person.'

***

'The company has made a personal transformation possible for me from a somewhat timid, average businessman to more of a spiritual manager. My learning question this year is: I want to learn how to become a spiritual manager.

'Such a leader is sensitive and sensible and not a mechanistic leader who leads from the perspective of his own ego. In this way I am able to get the best out of myself and others, which increases my self confidence and in fact achieves better results.

'As our company is also just a normal company and not just a movement of freedom fighters, we experience the good and the bad together, but it is still a wonderful company and helps me to work towards our ideals in life.'

***

'I cannot separate this from two other worlds in which I have worked: the political-governmental where I spent eighteen years and the academic world where I worked for thirty-one years.

'In the political and governmental worlds I connected with the ideal to make this world a better place. That touched me deeply. The key concept in those worlds was power in Weber's sense: *die Möglichkeit/Vermögen Wirklichkeit in Bewegung zu setzen* (the possibility/ability to put reality into motion).

'The shadow side to this is that all power has the tendency to corrupt. I had had enough when the tension between the ideal and reality became so big that the ideal tended towards cynicism.

'Within the university I felt a spiritual connection with wonder and admiration at creation. I wanted to understand it and that connected me to a world in which that is the highest goal. In a spiritual sense it was all about wonder and curiosity. But for some time now there have been many dark sides to that spiritual ground, because contrary to their original calling, universities strive for money and competitive power. I had had enough of this world because of the intense loneliness in which those people ultimately exist.

'After these experiences this company feels like paradise. What fascinated me from the beginning was the authentic dedication of all managers in the organization to honour and serve its goals. *To be of service* is what I connect with here. But what gives me immense daily pleasure is that I feel more whole in this organization. *Wholeness* means that I can be the way I am. Qualities of mine which were not used in other working environments are allowed to be: playfulness, being of service, curiosity, dexterity, longing, friendship and so on. Where in other offices I always had to wear a mask of functionality to show my dedication to the meaning of the organization, here I feel seen and accepted, bigger than in other offices, closer to my destiny, happier and more grounded.'

***

'A key phrase within my spiritual connection with the company is its motto "The client is yourself". It is a sentence which can be misunderstood and even misused in many ways, but I understand it as "Love thy neighbour as thyself". What is dominant in this parallelism of the client and the consultant is that theirs is not a functional relationship but one of complete persons. And so a lot of attention in our work is focused on the client's quest for his or her destiny. It is a search for the deep values which motivate a client's behaviour.

***

'I have read quite a few self-help books. I knew all about positive thinking, that you should act out of your own strength, that neuro-linguistic programming tricks work, etc.

'At first the stories the group leaders told seemed to be only optimistic words, a dream which perhaps I hoped to realize someday, but which was not really for me. I wanted to believe them but did not know how to go about it.

'If I could find my own way, if I finally started using my unique qualities, then suddenly my letter of application would be taken out of the enormous pile and the resulting job interview would lead to success. Yes, wonderful, but how to find the way? How do I know what makes me unique? How do I know my métier? And above all: when would I dare to follow that path and choose to ignore all the side ways? When would I dare to believe in myself?

'Somewhere in all those months of conversations in groups and with my coach, I began to realize that something was happening. I usually felt happy and strong after a session, and knew that I could make a difference in the group and my immediate environment, and perhaps in the rest of the world. And that feeling stayed with me for ever longer periods of time. The stories of the phoenix rising out of its ashes, the descriptions of the growing process of a rose, the drawings I made and analysed, to hear from a group member that I started to shine when I talked about a certain topic, to discover together with others what my deeper motives were, all these seeds slowly started to sprout. I suddenly discovered that all the stories about "standing in your strength" and "flow" were not as vague as I thought. I experienced that if I dared to make a choice and followed the path that seemed made for me, things just started happening. My CV was read, I was called, I received my first commission. Surprise, surprise, it works! This is it! This is what they mean! I think that everyone could benefit enormously from this process. It taught me to believe in myself, I took steps I would never have dared to take, or could not take before.'

***

'Rabbi Zusya said shortly before his death: "In heaven they will not ask me why I wasn't Moses, they will ask me why I wasn't Zusya." (Martin Buber)

'In my work I see this: one points at what is and not at what should be or has to be. The challenge is the search to develop a person: to bring this person into contact with his source, his personal qualities, and to give this form, with soul and passion.

'Development and personal growth hurts sometimes. To develop is to unfold and to see the resistance within you. It is similar to the process of a snake shedding its old skin when it needs a new one: it is hard work and when you are working you are vulnerable. In essence, the work on yourself is to reconnect heaven and earth: to be open for the creative impulse and to give it a form.

'Occasionally people are not open enough to receive an impulse: all fears, desires, emotions and expectations are barriers. One is not in the line of heaven and earth and it is impossible to create. The way of man is connecting the creative force of heaven with the receiving, shaping power of earth. We stand exactly between heaven and earth, literally and figuratively, and it is our spiritual road in life to connect these.'

We have been delighted to find that so many other people in all fields of business share our view that putting principles into practice, sometimes at an apparent cost to themselves, is the most profitable course of action for themselves and others.

In the last chapter, we shall propose some practical measures by which you, the reader, can put these principles into practice in your work and in your life.

CHAPTER 13 - THE WAY FORWARD

We have set before you a picture of a moral manager who through his or her efforts is able to develop and grow and to create the conditions for others to do the same. Our basic premise is that a moral manager is good and true, working from fine principles, not compromising these values the sake of expediency.

We have attempted to show examples of how this way of dealing with the activities of business works equally well in life outside the business world. The final step is to summarize for you some of the suggestions as to how you can begin to think, speak and act as a moral manager. This is where the work begins.

We said at the outset that first it is necessary to learn how to manage yourself before you can be an effective manager of other people. So that is the place to start.

Self-examination and self-discipline

All of us have established particular patterns of thought, speech and action that are not easily changed. It is possible to change but to do so requires will and a resolution. This determination to change can come about when we are presented with a clear picture of the ideal and when we have compared our behaviour against this model and found it wanting.

Underlying the action plan are principles and good practices, which will bring to bear your own consciousness and power on each business situation. The aim is to focus the attention so that heart and mind are not distracted by old habits and mechanical ways of thinking and feeling.

1. Observe yourself and others carefully. Be honest in your self-assessment and the evaluation of others. Maintain an open mind and avoid criticism at all costs.

2. When making a decision:

   Listen – with full attention so that you can be sure you understand the actual conditions of the moment;

   Reflect – Let the mind and heart approach the decision from a position of rest and stillness;

   Respond – respond fully and courageously with careful regard for the effect of your response on others.

3. Assess your individual value system in the context of universal principles and cultural values.

   What are your five most precious values; the ones that dwell in the heart and which colour and influence all your decisions?

   In the context of business what are the values that you will use as the basis for your thoughts, words and actions? If they are different from your personal values, know why they are different.

   Assess the level of the moral hierarchy at which you are operating and assess whether that is appropriate.

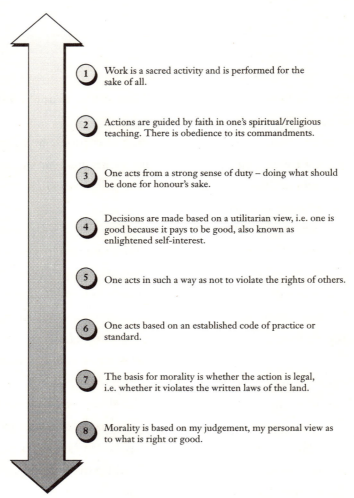

1. Work is a sacred activity and is performed for the sake of all.

2. Actions are guided by faith in one's spiritual/religious teaching. There is obedience to its commandments.

3. One acts from a strong sense of duty – doing what should be done for honour's sake.

4. Decisions are made based on a utilitarian view, i.e. one is good because it pays to be good, also known as enlightened self-interest.

5. One acts in such a way as not to violate the rights of others.

6. One acts based on an established code of practice or standard.

7. The basis for morality is whether the action is legal, i.e. whether it violates the written laws of the land.

8. Morality is based on my judgement, my personal view as to what is right or good.

The Moral Hierarchy

With these principles and practices in mind, you can now develop an action plan to give specific direction to your energies.

The action plan

Step 1 Establish a culture of trust

How can you help to re-establish trust at all levels – trust in you, in your company, in your managers, trust in the business community? Here are some suggestions:

1. Begin by being trustworthy – set an example. This can be best accomplished by bringing these great statements of the wise to life in your day-to-day business dealings:

> Love thy neighbour as thyself.
> Do unto others as you would have them do unto you.
> My word is my bond.

2. Follow the practical suggestions offered in Chapter 6 in establishing trust:

Be courageous	Let go of fear, take some risk. Do not hesitate to do what you know is right. Stand up against wrong.
Be honest and clear	Don't skirt round the difficult issues. Be straight about expectations.
Be open	Don't hide problems; share information and knowledge.
Be selfless	Take care of everyone else. Be willing to sacrifice your own interests.
Communicate effectively	Speak when it is appropriate, listen carefully and fully, and learn all the time.
Go the extra mile	Try to exceed the expectations of

	others; provide more than you have to.
Acknowledge efforts	Give praise and thanks where they are due.
Be fair	Seek the solution that is equitable for all.
Be consistent	Adhere constantly to true principles of thought, speech and action.
Discriminate	Discern the truth in a situation and act on it. To do this you have to be in the present and ignore pre-conceptions.

3. Maintain equanimity in adversity:

If you try to put our suggestions into practice, you are bound to meet substantial opposition. The first place that the resistance will be felt is within you. The temptation to cut corners, to take the easy way will be felt. Secondly you may meet resistance from others, such as colleagues, customers, management. For trust to be established considerable patience and determination will be required. It is important that the obstacles be met in a balanced way.

We suggest that you review Kipling's poem 'If' (page 72) and try to put into practice the values described in the verses, especially 'to treat success and failure, those two impostors just the same'.

Step 2 Engage fully both the head and the heart

This means the full use of the rational and emotional faculties, again in a balanced way. This can be facilitated by:

1. Being more acutely aware of your
- Intentions – What is my real motivation? To what or whom is this action dedicated?
- Attention – Am I acting in the present moment or on the basis of habit (the past) or imaginings (the future)?
- Retention – Am I taking too much credit and not recognizing the contributions of others? Can I surrender

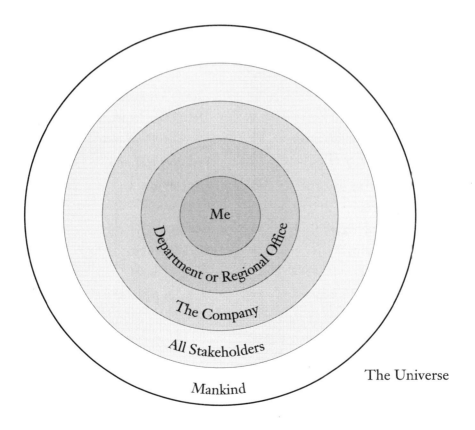

these claims?

2. Widening the circles of compassion in your life to embrace an ever expanding world. Act for the sake of family, company, nation and mankind. Keep expanding your view.

3. Fulfilling your duty of care to your 'stakeholders'. In your business this includes: customers, employees, senior management, suppliers, shareholders, the community, society at large.

4. Maintaining balance in the decisions you make. Acknowledge that there is a choice, be aware of the tendency to repeat old patterns and engage in quiet reflection. Let the knowledge arise to meet the need of the moment.

Here are the areas to watch:

Command/control	vs	Caring/compassion
Doing	vs	Delegating/empowering
Financial performance	vs	Social responsibility
Logical thinking	vs	Intuitive response
Risk aversion	vs	Innovation
Tradition	vs	Change
Teaching	vs	Learning
Maintaining	vs	Creating new
Discipline	vs	Love
Trust in technology	vs	Trust in people

Step 3 Serve, serve, serve

1. Ask yourself these questions:

- Am I committed to serving the common good, that is to say, the good of all?

- If so, then what is the next step I can take?

2. Remember that in assessing objectively the quality of service, three factors are important:

- The alignment of the motives and values of the seller and the buyer.
- The degree to which both parties (buyer and seller) are actually in the present moment i.e. attentive to what is happening.
- An honest acknowledgement of their respective contributions.

3. Examine all the processes in your organization to see whether their focus is on service.

Step 4 Be creative and put wealth in perspective

1. Begin all activities from stillness and return to that stillness upon completion.

2. Establish in your organization these steps for the creation of wealth

- Identify the need.
- Apply conscious effort.
- Work according to principle.
- Act with integrity - in the moment.
- Teamwork-give praise generously.
- Surrender personal limitations.
- Work in service of all.

3. Assess your personal ideas and attitude about wealth.

4. Remember the guidance of the wise:

- Nothing to excess.

- Seek the golden mean.
- Refine your sense of discrimination to decide what is enough.

Step 5 Allow virtue to be your guide

1. Remind yourself about the true dignity and nature of a human being. Do not be deceived by the clouds of ignorance that cover the sun of your true nature.

2. Remember the three functions of a manager: leading, organizing and teaching and apply as appropriate in the moment.

3. Remember to act from the four universal principles:

    Truth – Speak the truth in all situations, but without giving offence.

    Love – Care, service and benevolence for all.

    Justice – Do to others as you would have them do to you, serve to be served, respect to be respected, obey to be obeyed, be loyal to win loyalty.

    Freedom – Act in such a way as to be free from fear, pride, selfishness, arrogance and dependence on the opinion of others.

    Observe how the fine qualities and behaviours manifest naturally when these principles are your guide.

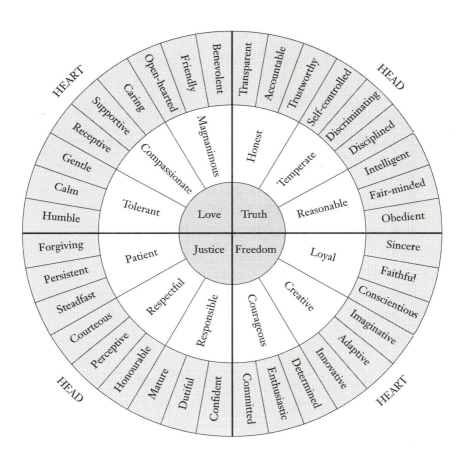

Step 6 Start on your journey of discovery

Recognize that in order to progress you must embark on a journey of discovery that requires steady individual resolve and the presence of good company along the way.

Step 7 Follow the road map to principles and profits

The road map begins with an organization that has:

1. Agreed foundation principles and values that need to be agreed, communicated and lived.

Agreement on these principles manifests as:

2. Consistent internal policies and standards recognized by all to be fair and responsive to the needs of both the company and the employees.

This results in:

3. A high level of employee and management satisfaction with high morale and more energy available for the business.

Thus enabling:

4. High productivity and enthusiasm a strong team spirit and a disciplined work pattern.

The result is:

5. High quality service delivered: reliable, assured, responsive, effective

Consequently:

6. A high level of customer satisfaction is ensured, producing customers who are loyal to the company.

This leads to:

7. Profits and growth.

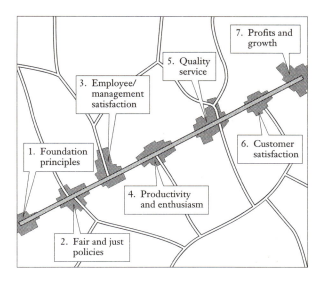

Conclusion

Is it possible to conduct business according to true principles *and* still be successful? We hope that we have demonstrated not only that it is possible but that this is the natural way to find happiness and satisfaction in business life, to assure the prosperity and longevity of your business, to engender good relations with your colleagues, customers, suppliers and investors and creatively to serve your community, nation and humankind.

We hope too that the fine moral principles and practical advice that we have presented will enable you to feel sufficiently confident to proceed on your own journey. The stories from so many like-minded people working around the world will, we trust, be inspiring for you as they have been for us.

To be a moral manager is simply to live naturally. To be what we truly are means that we need to stop making mistakes, and stay with the truth. If you sincerely try to put these principles into practice, you will find resistance, from within yourself and from others, but if you persevere, amazing things will happen. Try it: you will come to love your work.

We wish you good fortune on the way and a profitable outcome.

REFERENCES

Abu Said A'bil Khair (1992) *Rubaiyat*, Sharib Press

Accountancy Age (2005) 'Unilever calls for halt to reforms', November issue

Alsop, Ronald J. (2005) *The 18 Immutable Laws of Corporate Reputation*, Kogan Page

Aristotle, (1995 edn.) *Nichomachean Ethics*, The Complete Works of Aristotle, Princeton University Press

Armstrong, Dr James, (2005) 'The common good', unpublished course notes, School of Economic Science, London

Ashvagosha, *Buddhacharita*, www.indiaheritage.com

(Sri) Aurobindo (1995) *The Eternal Wisdom*, Sri Auribindo Ashram Publications

Azmi, Dr Sabahuddin (2005) 'An Islamic Approach to Business Ethics', (web article). www.renaissance.com.pk/tonevi.html

Babylonian Talmud, Shabbath, www.bibletools.org

Bahá'u'lláh (1976) *Gleanings from the Writings of Bahá'u'lláh*, Wilmette: Baha'i Publishing Trust

Bayot, Jennifer (2005) 'Ex-WorldCom officer gets 5 years in prison', *New York Times*, 11 August

(The) Bhagavad Gita, (1977), trans. Alladi Mahadeva Sastry, Samata Books

Bloxham, Eleanor and John M Nash (2005) *The Corporate Governance Alliance Digest* (monthly newsletter)

Blunden, Dr Brian, OBE, (2004) presentation, 'Ethics and profitability', Informal talk given in London, October 2004

Boethius, (1998 edn.) *The Consolation of Philosophy*, ed. V.E. Watts, Folio Society

Boldt, Laurence G. (1993) *Zen and the Art of Making a Living*, Penguin Books

Boyes, Roger (2005) 'BMW bribes expose tide of corruption', *The Times*, 29 July

Bunson, Matthew (ed.) (1997) *The Dalai Lama's Book of Wisdom*, Rider Books

Butcher, Sarah (2005) 'Recovery plan', *People Management*, 28 July

Byrne, Colin (2004) 'Your priceless asset', *Management Training*, November issue

CapGemini Article (2005) first appeared in *Le Monde*, quoted in the *Financial Times*, 17 October

Carlyle, Thomas (1966 edn.) *On Heroes, Hero Worship and Heroes in History*, University of Nebraska Press

Catholic Bishops of England and Wales, report, (1996) 'The Common Good'

Chopra, Deepak (1994) *7 Spiritual Steps to Success*, Ambler-Allen Publishing

Churches Together in Britain and Ireland, report (2005) 'Prosperity with a Purpose: exploring the ethics of affluence'

Churchill, Winston (2002 edn.) *Their Finest Hour – The Second World War*, Rosetta Books

Cicero (1971 edn.) *Selected Works*, trans. Michael Grant, Penguin Classics

Collins, James C. and Jerry I. Porras (1997) *Built to Last – Successful Habits of Visionary Companies*, HarperBusiness

Confucius (1971 edn.) *Analects*, trans. James Legge, Dover Publications

Council of Churches for Britain and Ireland, report (1997) 'Unemployment and the Future of Work'

Cox, Christopher (2005) *Wall Street Journal*, 15 September

Cullingford, Martin (2000) 'Companies look for moral support', *The Times*, 7 September

Denning, Steve (2004) 'Organizational and business storytelling in the news', www.stevedenning.com, 20 April

Dewhurst, Philip (2005) 'Trust between citizens' (lecture), RSA

Duncan, Gary (2005) 'World leaders are stuck in moral maze', *The Times Economic Agenda*, 31 January

Epictetus (1995 edn.) *The Art of Living*, ed. Sharon Lebell, Harper Books

Ficino, Marsilio (1978-1984) *The Letters of Marsilio Ficino*, Volumes 1–5, Shepheard Walwyn

Forstater, Mark (ed.) (2000) *The Spiritual Teachings of Marcus Aurelius*, Hodder & Stoughton

Franklin, Benjamin (1996) *The Art of Virtue*, George L Ross(ed), Choice Skills

Gallup Poll (2001) 'Religion and the aftermath of 9/11'

Gandhi, Mahatma (2003) *Indian Wisdom–365 Days*, Thames and Hudson

Geary, Rev. James (1977) *De Miseria Humane Conditions*, Catholic University Press of America

Gibbon, Edward (1977) *Decline and Fall of the Roman Empire*, J.M. Dent

Goethe, Johann Wolfgang von, wwwquoteworld.org

Greenleaf, Robert (1970) *The Servant as Leader*, Robert Greenleaf

Hadith Muslim. Imam 71-2, USC-MSA Compendium of Muslim Texts, www.usc.edu/dept/MSA

Halpern, David (2005) 'Trust in business', (lecture), RSA, April

Handy, Charles (1997) 'The search for meaning', *Leader to Leader*, Summer issue

Higgin, Graham (ed.) *Porcupines – a Philosophical Anthology*, Allan Lane, The Penguin Press, 1999.

Horace (1994 edn.) *Odes*, trans. David West, Oxford

Huntsman, B.W. (ed.) (1969) *Wisdom is One*, Vincent Stewart and John M. Watkins

Independent (2004) 'Prozac, Nation, UK', 30 March

Institute of Business Ethics (2003) Study of FTSE 250 Companies

Institute of Business Ethics, Lectures:

    Dewhurst, Philip 'Trust Between Citizens', April 2005

    Halpern, David 'Trust in Business April 2005

International Communications Training Institute (2004) 'British and Chinese values and attitudes'

Jefferson, Thomas (1977 edn.) *The Portable Thomas Jefferson*, ed. Peterson, Merrill, Penguin Books

Johnson & Johnson website, www.jnj.com

Justinian, *Codex Justinianus*, www.fordham.edu

Kempis, Thomas A' (1995 edn.) *The Imitation of Christ*, Image Books

Kheng-Hor, Khoo (1997) *Sun Tzu and Management*, Pelanduk Publications

Kipling, Rudyard, 'If', in *One Hundred and One Famous Poems* Contemporary Books

Klesc, Raymond (2005) 'Ethics in Islam' (in four parts), *Muslim Executive & Expatriate Newsletter*

Lao Tse (1972 edn.) *The Sayings of Lao Tse*, trans. Lionel Giles, John Murray

Little, Arthur D. (2003) 'The business case for corporate responsibility' *Business in the Community*

Littlechild, Michael (2003/4), 'CSR – Highlights of the debate', European Business Forum, Winter

Livery Companies of the City of London (undated), *Some Rules for the Conduct of Life for the Use of Such Freemen of London as Take Apprentices*

Loyola, St Ignatius, *Prayer for Generosity*, www.appleseeds.org

MacLaren, Leon (1978), *Principles of Music*, unpublished thesis, School of Economic Science, London

MacLaren, Leon (1998), *The Machinery of Government*, The School of Philosophy, Sydney, Australia

The Mahabharata (1976) 12 Volumes trans. Kisari Mohan Ganguli, Munshiram Manoharlal Publications

MacKay, Charles (1995 edn.) *Extraordinary Popular Delusions and the Madness of Crowds*, Crown

Mann, Horace (1968) *Thoughts on the Business of Life*, Forbes

Melville-Ross, Tim (1999) 'New direction for the new generation', *Director*, Annual Convention

Mencken, H.L.(ed), *A New Dictionary of Quotations*, (1946), Alfred A. Knopf

Mersmann, Hans (ed.) (1972), *Letters of Wolfgang Amadeus Mozart*, Dover Publications

Minton, Andrew, and Blagg, Matthew (2004), *Corporate Integrity: the Strategic Reality*, Critical Eye Publications

Montesquieu, Baron de, *The Spirit of the Laws*, in Graham Higgin (ed.), *Porcupines – a Philosophical Anthology* (1999), Allan Lane, The Penguin Press

Mother Teresa, *In the Final Analysis*, Source unknown

Muller, Max (ed.) (1979) *Laws of Manu*, Motilal Banarsidass

Myers, Steven Lee (2005) 'In Russia, bribery is the cost of business', *New York Times*, 22 October

Newark College of Engineering (1960) 'Engineering as a discipline'

New York Times (2005) 'CEO pay' 3 April, cit. in *Corporate Governance Alliance Digest*, Bloxham

O'Neill, Dr Onora (2002) BBC Reith Lectures: 'A Question of Trust'

Overell, Stephen (2003) 'Great Leaders', *Financial Times*, 24 February

Ozaniec, Naomi (ed.), (1994) *Elements of the Egyptian Wisdom*, Element Books

Parliament of World Religions (1999) 'Towards a global ethic – an initial declaration'

Penn, William (1978) *Fruits of Solitude*, Friends United Press (US)

Phan, Dr Seamus (2005) 'Finding Asian roots of ethics in business' 27 March, at www.seamusphan.com

Plato (1937 edn.) *The Dialogues of Plato*, trans. B Jowett, Random House

Points of Light Foundation (1999) Study www.pointsoflight.org Organization promoting workplace volunteering

Pope, Alexander, (2004 edn.) *An Essay on Criticism*, RA Kessinger

Pope John Paul II (2005a) *In My Own Words*, Hodder & Stoughton

Pope John Paul II (2005b) *Memory and Identity*, Weidenfeld & Nicolson

'(The) Priceless Ingredient', document by E R Squibb & Sons, c. 1920, cited at www.ciadvertising.org

Pythagoras, *Golden Verses of Pythagoras*, www.ancienthistory.about.com

Purohit Swami (ed.) (1973) *The Geeta*, Faber and Faber

(The) Qu'ran (1998) trans. Dr Taqi-ud-Din Al-Hilali and Dr Muhsin Khan, Darussalam

Ramakrishna (1980 edn.) *The Gospel of Ramakrishna*, trans. Swami Nikhilananda), Ramakrishna-Vivekananda Center

Reps, Paul (ed.) (1957) *Zen Flesh, Zen Bones*, trans. Nyogen Senaki, Penguin Books

Rieu, E.V. (1973 edn.) *Dhammapada*, Penguin Classics

Roffey Park Institute (2004) Study 'In Search for Meaning at Work'

de Roover, Raymond (1967) *San Bernardino of Siena and Saint'Antonino of Florence: the Two Great Economic Thinkers of the Middle Ages*, Boston, MA Baker Library, Harvard Graduate School of Business Administration

Rumi, Jalaluddin (1975) *Teachings of Rumi*, ed. E.H. Whinfield, E.P. Dutton

Saraswati, Sri Shantananda (1965–92) unpublished conversations at School of Economic Science, London

Schumacher. E.F. (1979) *Good Work*, Harper Colophon Books.

Shakespeare, William (1964 edn.) The Folio Press Shakespeare, The Folio Society

Simms, Jane (2002) 'Corporate Social Responsibility (CSR)', *Director*, December issue

Skapinker, Michael (2005) 'Measures of success must go beyond financial results', *Financial Times*, 2 March

Snow, C.P. (1962) 'Magnanimity' (lecture), St Andrews University. Copy of text not dated

St. Benedict (1997) *The Rule of St Benedict*, trans. Abbot Parry, Gracewing

T'ai Shang Kan by Ying P'ien (1906) *Treatise of the Exalted One on Response and Retribution*, trans. Teitaro Suzuki and Dr. Paul Carus, The Open Court Publishing Co.

Tideman, Sander (2005) *Mind Over Matter*, Van Ede Foundation

Udanavarga, www.en.wikipedia.org

Welch, Jilly (1998) 'Creed is good', *People Management* 24 December

Witzel, Morgen (2004) 'Not for wealth alone: the rise of business ethics', *Financial Times* 'Mastering' series

Witzel, Morgen (2004) 'How Japan leapt into the modern age', *Managers before Management*

Wray, William (2005) *Sayings of the Buddha*, Capella

Yamamoto, Tsunetomo (2000 edn.) *Hagakure: The Book of the Samurai* trans. W.S. Wilson, Kodansha Europe

---

BIBLIOGRAPHY

Chapter One

Armstrong, Karen and Dr Khalid Hameed CBE
(2005),'Spirituality and global citizenship', RSA Hibbert Trust
Lecture, 30 June

Kay, John (1999), 'Ethics – The Role of Business in Society'
Lecture at Oxford University, 3 February 1998

Kennedy, Carol (2003), *From Dynasties to Dotcoms – the Rise, Fall
and Reinvention of British Business in the past 100 Years*, Director
Publications, Institute of Directors

Leewens, Hans (2002), 'A renaissance in modern management'
(essay), Van Ede Foundation

Melville-Ross, Tim (1997), 'Can business do more to project its
purpose and values?' *RSA Journal*, June

Ulrich, Peter and Thomas Maak, (1999) 'Business ethics – the
founding principles', European Business Forum

Winship, Michael (2003),'The Roots of the Scientific
WorldView', www.owenbarfield.com

Chapter Two

Armstrong, James, Ross Dixon and Simon Robinson (1999), *The
Decision Makers – Ethics for Engineers*, Thomas Telford Publishing

Cummins, Julian (1999), 'The teaching of business ethics', presentation, RSA Forum for Ethics in the workplace, 4 February

Henery, Michelle and Helen Rumbelow (2002), 'Business leaders
are spilt over Williams speech', *The Times*, 20 September

McCall, Catherine (1999), 'Rekindling the philosophical spirit',

RSA Journal, 3 April

Overell, Stephen (2003), 'Great leaders', *Financial Times*, 24 February

Rees-Mogg, William (2005), 'Dismal doubts: Why we're not a happy continent', *The Times*, April

Talbot, Marianne (1998), 'What are values?' lecture, RSA Forum for Ethics in the Workplace, 7 May

Tate, Dr Nicholas (1997), 'Values in the curriculum', *RSA Journal*, August/September

Trompenaars, Fons and Charles Hampden-Turner (1997), *Riding the Waves of Culture – Understanding Cultural Diversity in Business*, Nicholas Brealey Publishing

Watkins, Jon (2003), 'Spiritual guidance', *People Management*, 20 February

Wray, William (2005), *Philosophy Works – Accessing the Power of Great Ideas for a Happier Life*, Watkins Publishing

Chapter Three

Bennett, William J. (ed.) (1993, *The Book of Virtues – A Treasury of Great Moral Stories*, Simon & Schuster

Burke, Eugene (2005), 'The goal of integrity', *People Management*, 30 June

Cafaro, Philip (2004), The virtues of self-help', *Philosophy Now*, March/April

Duncan, Gary (2000), 'Morals can help to rebuild investor faith', *The Times: Economic Agenda*, 1 February

Grayling, Dr Anthony C., Dr Geoff Mulgan and Dr Theodore Zeldin (2004) 'Richer is not happier: a 21st century search for a good life', lecture, RSA, 11 February

Howard, Anthony (2005), 'Morality is on the march in our political system', *The Times: T2*, 22 March

Kidder, Rushworth (1999), 'Global ethics and individual responsibility', *RSA Journal*, 1 April

Morgan, Christopher (2005), 'Church finds faith in money', *Sunday Times*, 6 February

Oborne, Peter (2002), 'Debate:ethics versus enlightened self interest', *Human Resources Journal*, February

Radcliffe, David and Dr Theodore Zeldin (2004), 'The spirit of work: an exploration of ethical leadership', RSA Lecture – Annual CMI Lecture, 22 April

Runzo, Joseph and Nancy Martin (eds), (2001), *Ethics in the World Religions*, Oneworld Publications

Rushton, Kenneth (1998), 'Global ethics and the multinational corporation', RSA lecture, 3 December

Shlaes, Amity (2005), 'Moral action should be its own reward', *Financial Times*, 31 January

Tideman, Sander G (2005), 'Towards a new paradigm for business and economics', *Mind over Matter*, January

Vassallo, Philip (2004), 'Arête', *Philosophy Now*, March/April

Chapter Four

Bennett, Chris (2002), The Tao of Business Success, `Publisher-Her Business'

Burns, Kevin (2004), *Eastern Philosophy – The Greatest Thinkers and Sages from Ancient to Modern Times*, 2005, Arcturus Publishing Ltd

Gill, Robin (ed.) (2003), *The Cambridge Companion to Christian Ethics*, Cambridge University Press

Guptara, Professor Pradhu (1998), 'Ethics across cultures', *RSA*

Journal, Forum for Ethics in the Workplace, 2 April

Harney, John (2001), 'Zen communities of practice in western corporations', *Knowledge Management*, June

Kattih, Abdoulrahman (2004), 'Business Ethics in Islam', The Islamic Education and Services Institute

Koestline, Henry (1970), *What Jesus Said About It*, The New American Library

Kripalani, Krishna (ed.) (1972), *All Men are Brothers – Life and Thoughts of Mahatma Gandhi*, World Without War Publications, UNESCO

Mawdudi, Kriyananda, Swami (2004), *Material Success through Yoga Principles*, Ananda Sangha Publications

Kriyananda, Swami (2004), *Secrets of Success*, Ananda Sangha Publications

Linzey, Andrew (ed.), *The Sayings of Jesus*, Gerald Duckworth & Co Ltd

Naqi Baqirshahi, Ali, (2004), 'The Nature of Moral Values- The Light of Islam, A study of the views of Allamah Tabataba'I and Martyr Mutahhari', www.swipenet.se/islam/articles/moral-values

Piparaiya, Ram K. (2004), *Yoga of Work – Conversations with Sri Krishna*, Indusvista Editions

Sayyid Abul A'la (1991), *Let Us Be Muslims*, Islamic Foundation

Sen, Dr Sanat Kumar (2003), *The Ethical Relevance of Advaita Vedanta*, University of Northern Bengal

(The) Study Society (1987), *Good Company*

Swami, Shree Purohit and W.B. Yeats (eds) (1975), *The Ten Principal Upanishads*, Faber and Faber

Tigunait, Dr Pandit Rajmani (2002), 'Introduction to Indian philosophy', *Dawn*, Vol. 3. No 1

Chapter Five

Barnett, Anthony (1999), 'The Nice Man Cometh', *Director*, December

Browne, John M. (2004), 'Building an e-reputation', European Business Forum

Butcher, David and Penny Harvey (1999), 'Be upstanding', *People Management*, 30 June

Czerny, Anna (2004), 'Financial crime on the rise', *People Management*, 25 November

Doherty, Christian (2005), 'One good turn', *Real Financial*, July/August

FT 'Mastering' series (2005), 'Corporate Governance', 3 June.

Glover, Carol (2002), 'A common good', *People Management*, 10 October

Maitland, Alison (2003), 'No hiding place for the irresponsible business', *Financial Times Management*, 29 September

Murray, Sarah (2003), 'Technology factories face "sweatshops" probe', *Financial Times*, 29 September

Philpott, John (2003), 'The great stakeholder debate', *People Management*, 7 August

Pickard, Jane (2005), 'Social worker', *People Management*, 30 October

Toms, Michael (plus other contributors), (1997), *The Soul of Business*, Hay House

Walters, J. Donald & Swami Kriyananda, (1992) *Money Magnetism – How to Attract What You Need When You Need It*, Ananda Sangha Publications

Chapter Six

Asacker, Tom (2004). 'Ethics in the Workplace', Training &

Development, August.

Ashworth, Jon and Gary Duncan (2005), 'Fraud could deliver body blow to the national economy', *The Times*

Bickerton, Ian (2005), 'New code to "restore trust" in companies', *Financial Times*

Bolger, Joe and Sarah Butler (2005), 'Dixon tackles unethical firms', *The Times*

Bones, Chris (2005), 'Integrity is as important as ability', *Human Resources*, May

Elliott, John and Lauren Quantance (2003), 'Britain is getting less trusting', *Sunday Times*, 18 May

HR Magazine (2005), 'Fraud "is easy" claim employees', Editorial, December.

Jones, Gareth (1999), 'Look After Your Heart', *People Management*, 29 July.

Miller, Julie and Brian Bedford (2003), 'How to re-establish trust with core values', *People Management*, 18 December.

Myers, Steven Lee (2005), 'In Russia bribery is the cost of business', *New York Times*, 22 October

Parker, Andrew (2005) 'We have to prove our own quality', *Financial Times*, 21 July

Wapshott, Nicholas (2004), 'Liars and cheats give country built on hard work a bad name', *The Times*, 29 March

Chapter Seven

Accenture (2004), 'Accenture's overseas adventure volunteer schemes', *People Management*, 23 December.

Bonhoeffer, Dietrich (2002), 'How to be good', *Sunday Bulletin*, 13 October

Chana, Jasvinder Kaur (2005), 'Love and discipline leads to
Wahegur', *India Times*, April

Crammond, Joan (ed.) (2004), *Sheila Rosenberg – A Renaissance
Lady*, Godstow Press

Hackett, General Sir John (2000), 'On discovering the emotional
contract', *Farsight Management*

Wark, Penny (2003), 'You need emotion to be a winner', *The
Times: T2*, 26 February

Chapter Eight

Goodhart, David (2005), 'Liberals should beware of giving rights
to people who hate us', *Sunday Times*, 28 August

Gratton, Lynda (2002), 'A stock of options', *People Management*, 8
August

Hall, Amanda and Rupert Steiner (2005), 'Power went to
Messier's head,' *The Times*

The Times (2004), 'Have faith', 24 December.

Chapter Nine

Hampson, Stuart (1998), 'I like being an employee', *RSA Journal*,
Forum for Ethics in the Workplace, 2 April

Chapter Ten

Bayliss, Valerie (1998), 'Redefining work', *RSA Journal*, 2 April

Bennett, Rosemary (2000), 'Minister highlights long hours culture', *Financial Times*

Boldt, Laurence G. (1996), *How to Find the Work You Love*,
Penguin Books

(The) Dalai Lama (2003), Extract from 'How to Achieve

Happiness at Work', published in *The Times*, 7 October

Foster, Joanna (1999), 'National Work/Life Forum', Lecture, Forum for Ethics in the Workplace, 8 July

Girard, Lawrence Vijay (2004), *Flowing in the Workplace – A Guide to Personal and Professional Success*, Fruitgarden Publishing

Glover, Carol and Steven Smethurst (2003), 'Creativity is largely in the hands of the individual', *People Management*, 20 March

Merriden, Trevor (2002), 'Mutual', *Human Resources*, October

Mulgan, Geoff, Dr Anthony Grayling and Dr Theodore Zeldin (2004), 'What is the good life?', RSA lecture, 11 February

Reed, Jonathan (2003), 'Negative Pressure', *People Management*, 10 July

RSA Journal (1997), 'Redefining work',Editorial, June

Woolfrey, Celia (2005), 'Get up and go', *RSA Journal*, August

Chapter Eleven

Aldrich, Clark (2003), 'Leadership', *Training & Development*, March

Alimo-Metcalfe, Beverly and John Alban-Metcalfe (2002), 'The great and the good', *People Management*, 10 January

Arkin, Anat (2004), 'Bread and butler: great leaders serve their staff', *People Management*, 23 December

Ashdown, Paddy, Jack Cunningham and John Grigg (1999), 'Leadership into the 21st century', *The Times*, 9 February

Benjamin, Kim and Vikki Kunz (2004) 'It's good to talk', *Business XL*, September

Bodhananda, Swami (1994), *The Gita and Management*, Sambodh Foundation

Boddy, David (1999), *Marcilio Ficino on Leadership*, Farsight

Management

Collins, Jim (2002), 'The Great and the Good', *Director*, January

Corrigan, Paul (1999), *Shakespeare on Management – Leadership Lessons for Today's Managers*, Kogan Page.

Covey, Stephen (2002), Address to IOD Annual Convention by the Director.

Deverell, Lieutenant General J.F., OBE (1998), 'Can you teach leadership?', *RSA Journal*, 3 April.

Dearlove, Des (1999), 'Turning employees into leaders', *Human Resources*, October

Gillen, Terry (2003), 'Leadership training: how to give it practical impact', *Training Journal*, December

Greenhalgh, Leonard, Jay Conger, Donald Marchand and Andrew Ward (2002), 'Mastering leadership', *Financial Times*, Part 5, 29 November

Hodgson, Philip (1998), 'Leadership', *RSA Journal*, 3 April

Jackson, Michael (2005), 'Mind-set of a leader', *Business XL*, March

Jansen, Mark (1999), 'What makes a good leader?', *Enterprise*, March/April

Kriyananda, Swami (2005), *The Art of Supportive Leadership – A Practical Guide for People in Positions of Responsibility*, Ananda Sangha Publications

Leewens, Hans (2005), *On Courage – How to Do Justice to People, Things and Yourself*, Van Ede Foundation

May, Gary and Bill Kahnweiler (2002) 'Shareholder value: is there common ground?', *Training & Development*

Overell, Stephen (2003), 'The art of balancing imperatives', *Financial Times*, 29 September

Pitcher, Patricia (1999), 'Artists, craftsmen and technocrafts',
Training & Development, July

Rawlin, Joseph A. (2003), 'The myth of charismatic leaders',
Training & Development, March

Simms, Jane (2002), 'Is Britain being led astray?, *Director*, January

INDEX

activity and full life 226-7
anger, absence of 68
Aristotle 14, 66, 70, 158
arrogance 101
Art of War, The 101
Attar, Farid-uddin 69
attention 174-5
Aurelius, Marcus 67

Benardino of Siena, San 18-19
benevolence 85, 89, 139-44
Bhagavad Gita 69, 78
bibliography 274-83
Blackie, John Stuart 67
Boethius 16, 39
Britain, growth as world power 20-1
Buddhism 31, 34-5, 80-1, 83
business
    activities deplored 29
    China and Western ways 81-2
    contracting 189-90
    creativity 200-5
    customer support 191
    design 184-6
    development 184-6
    English as common language 27
    flourish in peacetime 33
    Japan 83-6
    key factors conducive to trade 13-14
    'love' word use 140-2
    market presentation 186-7
    negative publicity 29
    not trusted to regulate itself 94
    ordering 189-90
    pricing 187-8
    principles 90-3
    product delivery 190
    product installation 190
    product packaging 187
    public trust lost 112
    religious attitude 14-15
    role in society 13
    role to create wealth for community 30
    service at the heart 172, 183
    short term performance 164-5
    sport 37
    unethical 116
    wealth creation 205-9

caring and detachment 228
Carlyle, Thomas 71
caste system 77
charity 66
'charity principle' 91
China
    Buddhism 80-1
    Confucianism 31-2, 62, 64, 80, 82-3, 139, 152, 158
    morality 79-83
    negotiations within 25-6
    spiritual traditions 31-2
    values compared with British 80
    Western business ways 81-2
Churchill, Winston S 131, 228
Cicero 65, 71
class distinction 49
Common Good, The 75
'community' 130, 134
companies
    core values 94-5
    corporate social responsibility (CSR) 90-1, 92-3, 120, 134-5
    ethical codes 92-3, 108, 118
    foundation values 97-8
    mission statements 92, 108
    paternalistic responsibilities 91
    'property conception' 90
    reputation judgement 111
    'social entity conception' 90
    spirituality at work 95-7
    'triple bottom line' 92-3
    universal principles 97-8
    virtue circles 133-4
    visionary 94-5
compassion 68, 128-38
Confucius and Confucianism 31-2, 62, 64, 80, 82-3, 139, 152, 158
Consolation of Philosophy, The 16

contemptus mundi 16-17
contract 20, 47-8
Corporate Integrity: The Strategic Reality 119-20
corporate philanthropy 135-6
corporate social responsibility (CSR) 90-1, 92-3, 120
courage 64, 158-60, 242, 243
courtesy 165
cowardice 101
creativity 144, 200-5, 209-13, 213
cultures
    change to Eastern traditions 28
    clashes 27
    differences 24, 27
    dying 15
    flourishes when wealth increases 33
    group-oriented 50-1
    values 46-9
customer before company 123-4
customer needs triangle 174

decision making 253
detachment and not caring 228
Dhammapada 69
dignity 67
'dot-com' bubble 117

Ebbers, Bernie 157
efficiency and speed 230
18 *Immutable Laws of Corporate Reputation, The* 108
Einstein, Albert 131-2
emotional intelligence 219
emotions
    essentially the same in all 59-60
    excessive 101
    power 172-3
employees 127-8, 147-8, 150-1
Engineer's Oath 137-8English as common language 27
Epictetus 68
equanimity 69
executives
    applying rules to themselves 152
    compensation 149

failure, fear of 38
fairness 146-50
faith 65

'family' 129-30, 133
Ficino, Marsilio 19
forgiveness 66
foundation values
    courage 158-60
    freedom 224
    justice 222-3
    love 224
    loyalty 160-1
    magnanimity 162-3
    overview 97-8
    patience 164-5
    respect 165-7
    responsibility 167-70
    temperance 170
    tolerance 171
    truth 222-3
Franklin, Benjamin 61
freedom 69, 218, 224
freedom
    economic 155
    expression through independence 155-6
    moral value 89
    political 154-5
    virtue 154-8
friendship 70
full life and activity 226-7

Gandhi, Mahatma 67-8, 79, 131
generosity 67, 227-8
Gibbon, Edward 15
global
    communications 23
    interdependence of all countries 29
    operations 23
Golden Rule 45-6, 59
Good Work 209
graduation oath 137-8
greed 23, 40-1
Guilds 17

hadith 87
Hagakure 83-4
halal 86-7
haram 86-7
Hitopadesa 70
honesty 66, 234-8
honour 107, 108-10
hope 68

hospitality 70
humility 67

IF 71-3
India
    morality 77-9
    spiritual tradition 32-3, 34-5
    Vedic tradition 77
individual rights 50, 91. 92
Industrial Revolution 20-1
information and knowledge 226
Innocent III, Pope 16-17
integrity 118-24
intention 172-3
interdependence 156
International Spirit at Work award 243-4
investors, fairness to 149
Islam
    charity 87
    tradition 32
    usury 27
    values 86-8

Japan
    attention to quality 22
    Buddhism 83
    business 83-6
    morality 83-6
Jefferson, Thomas 65
jewellery business example 113-15
John Paul II, Pope 28, 63, 69
Johnson & Johnson 'Credo' 93-4
Judaeo-Christian
    morality 74-6
    tradition 31
    values 74-6, 154
    justice 65, 89, 146-54, 217, 222-3
Justinian 147

Kempis, Thomas A 64
Kipling, Rudyard 71-3
knowledge and information 226

Lao Tse 63, 227
little lies 234
Livery companies 17-18
love 69, 89, 126-8, 217, 224
loyalty 160-1

magnanimity 162-3

management theory and techniques 22
manners, good 143, 165
Merchant of Venice 19-20
mind
    essentially the same in all 59-60
Mind over Matter 126-7
money and wealth 228
Montesquieu, Baron de 20
moral dilemmas 100-2
moral effectiveness 152-3
moral hierarchy 54-9, 253-4
moral manager
    action plan 255
    actions 218-19, 252
    balance necessary 219-20
    becoming 144
    caring and compassion 220
    choosing correctly 230-2
    command and control 220
    creativity 259-60
    creativity and happiness 209-13
    decision making 253
    equity 147
    fairness 147
    foundation values 221-5
    freedom 218
    full use of faculties 256-8
    functions 215-17
    guiding principles 216-18
    individual value system 253
    justice 217
    leadership 214-15, 216
    love 217
    mistakes commonly made 226-30
    organizer 216
    profile 221
    self-discipline 252-3
    self-examination 252-3
    service, service, service 258-9
    summary 261-4
    teacher 216
    trust culture 255-6
    truth 217
    universal principles 260
    virtue as guide 260
    virtue circles 257, 261
    virtues as basis 171
    way forward 252-64
    wealth creation 206-9
moral principles 54, 97
moral purity 152-3